INSTRUCTOR-LED TRAINING

APPROVED COURSEWARE

Step
by
Step
Courseware

Microsoft®
FrontPage® 2000

Core Skills Student Guide

ActiveEducation™

PUBLISHED BY
Microsoft Press
A Division of Microsoft Corporation
One Microsoft Way
Redmond, Washington 98052-6399

Library of Congress Cataloging-in-Publication Data
Microsoft FrontPage 2000 Step by Step Courseware Core Skills Student Guide / ActiveEducation.
     p. cm.
   Includes index.
   ISBN 0-7356-0703-6 -- ISBN 0-7356-0975-6
   1. Microsoft FrontPage. 2. Web sites--Design. I. ActiveEducation (Firm)

  TK5105.8885.M53 M536 1999
  005.7'2--dc21   99-050358

Printed and bound in the United States of America.

1 2 3 4 5 6 7 8 9   WCWC   5 4 3 2 1 0

Distributed in Canada by Penguin Books Canada Limited.

A CIP catalogue record for this book is available from the British Library.

Microsoft Press books are available through booksellers and distributors worldwide. For further information about international editions, contact your local Microsoft Corporation office or contact Microsoft Press International directly at fax (425) 936-7329. Visit our Web site at mspress.microsoft.com.

For ActiveEducation:
Managing Editor: Ron Pronk
Series Editor: Kate Dawson
Project Editor: R. Lee White
Writers: Scott Palmer, Ron Pronk, Dave Versdahl
Production/Layout: Linda Savell, Valerie Hall,
 Tracey Varnell
Technical Editors: Nicole French, Kris Gallaugher,
 Lorrie Werner
Indexer: Kathy Strange
Proofreaders: Holly Freeman, Jennifer Jordan

For Microsoft Press:
Acquisitions Editor: Susanne M. Forderer
Project Editor: Jenny Moss Benson

Contents

Course Overview

Welcome to the *Step by Step Courseware* series for Microsoft Office 2000 and Microsoft Windows 2000 Professional. This series facilitates classroom learning, letting you develop competence and confidence in using an Office application or operating system software. In completing courses taught with *Step by Step Courseware*, you learn to use the software productively and discover how to make the software work for you. This series addresses core-level and expert-level skills in Microsoft Word 2000, Microsoft Excel 2000, Microsoft Access 2000, Microsoft Outlook 2000, Microsoft FrontPage 2000, and Microsoft Windows 2000 Professional.

The *Step by Step Courseware* series provides:

■ A time-tested, integrated approach to learning.

■ Task-based, results-oriented learning strategies.

■ Exercises based on business scenarios.

■ Complete preparation for Microsoft Office User Specialist (MOUS) certification.

■ Attractive student guides with full-featured lessons.

■ Lessons with accurate, logical, and sequential instructions.

■ Comprehensive coverage of skills from the basic to the expert level.

■ Review of core-level skills provided in expert-level guides.

■ A CD-ROM with practice files.

A Task-Based Approach Using Business Scenarios

The *Step by Step Courseware* series builds on the strengths of the time-tested approach that Microsoft developed and refined for its Step by Step series. Even though the Step by Step series was created for self-paced training, instructors have long used it in the classroom. For the first time, this popular series has been adapted specifically for the classroom environment. By studying with a task-based approach, you learn more than just the features of the software. You learn how to accomplish real-world tasks so that you can immediately increase your productivity using the software application.

The lessons are based on tasks that you might encounter in the everyday work world. This approach allows you to quickly see the relevance of the training. The task-based focus is woven throughout the series, including lesson organization within each unit, lesson titles, and scenarios chosen for practice files.

An Integrated Approach to Training

The *Step by Step Courseware* series distinguishes itself from other series on the market with its consistent delivery and completely integrated approach to learning across a variety of print and online training media. With the addition of the *Step by Step Courseware* series, which supports classroom instruction, the *Step by Step* training suite now provides a flexible and unified training solution.

Print-Based Self-Training in the Step by Step Training Suite

The proven print-based series of stand-alone *Step by Step* books has consistently been the resource that customers choose for developing software skills on their own.

Online Training in the Step by Step Training Suite

For those who prefer online training, the *Step by Step Interactive* products offer highly interactive online training in a simulated work environment, complete with graphics, sound, video, and animation delivered to a single station (self-contained installation), local area network (LAN), or intranet. *Step by Step Interactive* has a network administration module that allows a training manager to track the progress and quiz results for students using the training. For more information, see *www.mspress.microsoft.com*.

Preparation for Microsoft Office User Specialist (MOUS) Certification

This series has been certified as approved courseware for the Microsoft Office User Specialist certification program. Students who have completed this training are prepared to take the related MOUS exam. By passing the exam for a particular Office application, students demonstrate proficiency in that application to their employers or prospective employers. Exams are offered at participating test centers. For more information, see *www.mous.net*.

A Sound Instructional Foundation

All products in the *Step by Step Courseware* series apply the same instructional strategies, closely adhering to adult instructional techniques and reliable adult learning principles. Lessons in the *Step by Step Courseware* series are presented in a logical, easy-to-follow format, helping you find information quickly and learn as efficiently as possible. To facilitate the learning process, each lesson follows a consistent structure.

Designed for Optimal Learning

The following "Lesson Features" section shows how the colorful and highly visual series design makes it easy for you to see what to read and what to do when practicing new skills.

Lessons break training into easily assimilated sessions. Each lesson is self-contained, and lessons can be completed in sequences other than the one presented in the table of contents. Sample files for the lessons don't depend on completion of other lessons. Sample files within a lesson assume only that you are working sequentially through a complete lesson.

The *Step by Step Courseware* series features:

- **Lesson objectives.** Objectives clearly state the instructional goals for each lesson so that you understand what skills you will master. Each lesson objective is covered in its own section, and each section or topic in the lesson is covered in a consistent way. Lesson objectives preview the lesson structure, helping you grasp key information and prepare for learning skills.

- **Informational text for each topic.** For each objective, the lesson provides easy-to-read, technique-focused information.

- **Hands-on practice.** Numbered steps give detailed, step-by-step instructions to help you learn skills. The steps also show results and screen images to match what you should see on your computer screen. The accompanying CD contains sample files used for each lesson.

- **Full-color illustrations in color student guides.** Illustrated screen images give visual feedback as you work through exercises. The images reinforce key concepts, provide visual clues about the steps, and give you something to check your progress against.

- **MOUS icon.** Each section or sidebar that covers a MOUS certification objective has a MOUS icon in the margin at the beginning of the section. The number of the certification objective is also listed.

- **Tips.** Helpful hints and alternate ways to accomplish tasks are located throughout the lesson text.

- **Important.** If there is something to watch out for or something to avoid, this information is added to the lesson and indicated with this heading.

- **Sidebars.** Sidebars contain parenthetical topics or additional information that you might find interesting.

- **Margin notes** Margin notes provide additional related or background information that adds value to the lesson.

- **Button images in the margin.** When the text instructs you to click a particular button, an image of the button and its label appear in the margin.

- **Lesson Glossary.** Terms with which you might not be familiar are defined in the glossary. Terms in the glossary appear in boldface type within the lesson and are defined upon their first use within lessons.

- **Quick Quiz.** You can use the short-answer Quick Quiz questions to test or reinforce your understanding of key topics within the lesson.

Lesson Features

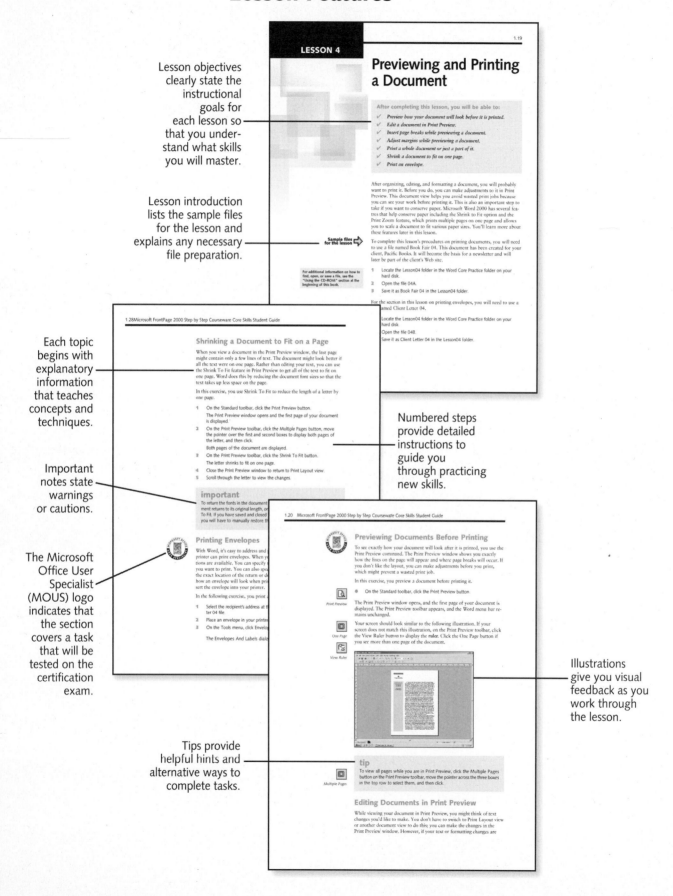

Lesson objectives clearly state the instructional goals for each lesson so that you understand what skills you will master.

Lesson introduction lists the sample files for the lesson and explains any necessary file preparation.

Each topic begins with explanatory information that teaches concepts and techniques.

Important notes state warnings or cautions.

The Microsoft Office User Specialist (MOUS) logo indicates that the section covers a task that will be tested on the certification exam.

Tips provide helpful hints and alternative ways to complete tasks.

Numbered steps provide detailed instructions to guide you through practicing new skills.

Illustrations give you visual feedback as you work through the lesson.

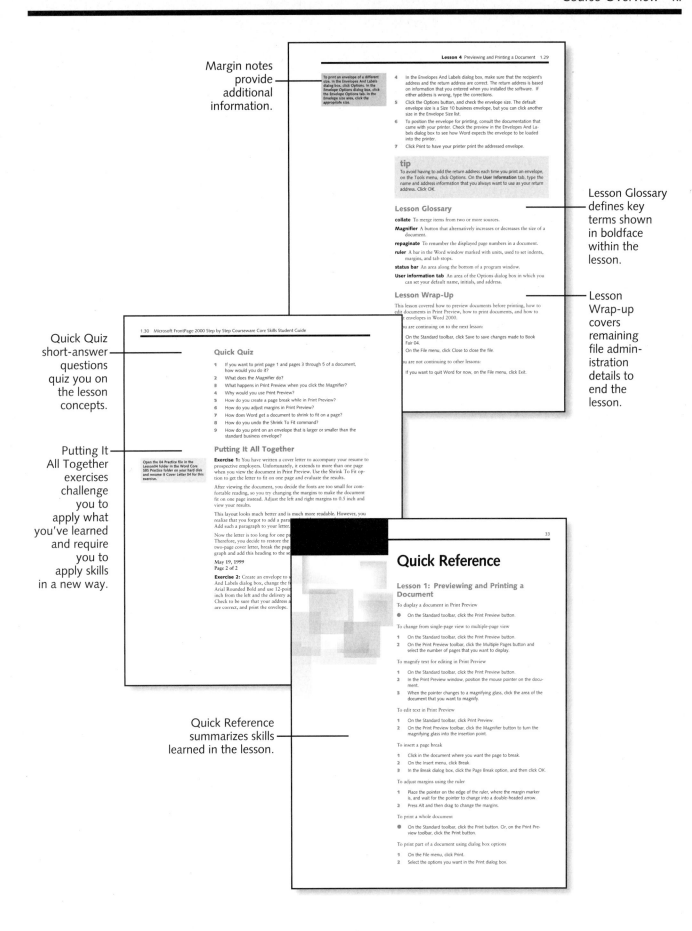

Margin notes provide additional information.

Lesson Glossary defines key terms shown in boldface within the lesson.

Lesson Wrap-up covers remaining file administration details to end the lesson.

Quick Quiz short-answer questions quiz you on the lesson concepts.

Putting It All Together exercises challenge you to apply what you've learned and require you to apply skills in a new way.

Quick Reference summarizes skills learned in the lesson.

Lesson 4 Previewing and Printing a Document   1.29

> To print an envelope of a different size, in the Envelopes And Labels dialog box, click Options. In the Envelope Options dialog box, click the Envelope Options tab. In the Envelope size area, click the appropriate size.

4   In the Envelopes And Labels dialog box, make sure that the recipient's address and the return address are correct. The return address is based on information that you entered when you installed the software. If either address is wrong, type the corrections.

5   Click the Options button, and check the envelope size. The default envelope size is a Size 10 business envelope, but you can click another size in the Envelope Size list.

6   To position the envelope for printing, consult the documentation that came with your printer. Check the preview in the Envelopes And Labels dialog box to see how Word expects the envelope to be loaded into the printer.

7   Click Print to have your printer print the addressed envelope.

tip
To avoid having to add the return address each time you print an envelope, on the Tools menu, click Options. On the **User Information** tab, type the name and address information that you always want to use as your return address. Click OK.

Lesson Glossary

collate To merge items from two or more sources.

Magnifier A button that alternatively increases or decreases the size of a document.

repaginate To renumber the displayed page numbers in a document.

ruler A bar in the Word window marked with units, used to set indents, margins, and tab stops.

status bar An area along the bottom of a program window.

User information tab An area of the Options dialog box in which you can set your default name, initials, and address.

Lesson Wrap-Up

This lesson covered how to preview documents before printing, how to edit documents in Print Preview, how to print documents, and how to print envelopes in Word 2000.

If you are continuing on to the next lesson:

On the Standard toolbar, click Save to save changes made to Book Fair 04.
On the File menu, click Close to close the file.

If you are not continuing to other lessons:

If you want to quit Word for now, on the File menu, click Exit.

1.30   Microsoft FrontPage 2000 Step by Step Courseware Core Skills Student Guide

Quick Quiz

1   If you want to print page 1 and pages 3 through 5 of a document, how would you do it?
2   What does the Magnifier do?
3   What happens in Print Preview when you click the Magnifier?
4   Why would you use Print Preview?
5   How do you create a page break while in Print Preview?
6   How do you adjust margins in Print Preview?
7   How does Word get a document to shrink to fit on a page?
8   How do you undo the Shrink To Fit command?
9   How do you print on an envelope that is larger or smaller than the standard business envelope?

Putting It All Together

> Open the 04 Practice file in the Lesson04 folder in the Word Core SBS Practice folder on your hard disk and rename it Cover Letter 04 for this exercise.

Exercise 1: You have written a cover letter to accompany your resume to prospective employers. Unfortunately, it extends to more than one page when you view the document in Print Preview. Use the Shrink To Fit option to get the letter to fit on one page and evaluate the results.

After viewing the document, you decide the fonts are too small for comfortable reading, so you try changing the margins to make the document fit on one page instead. Adjust the left and right margins to 0.5 inch and view your results.

This layout looks much better and is much more readable. However, you realize that you forgot to add a para[...] Add such a paragraph to your letter.

Now the letter is too long for one pa[...] Therefore, you decide to restore the [...] two-page cover letter, break the page[...] graph and add this heading to the se[...]

May 19, 1999
Page 2 of 2

Exercise 2: Create an envelope to s[...] And Labels dialog box, change the f[...] Arial Rounded Bold and use 12-poin[...] inch from the left and the delivery a[...] Check to be sure that your address a[...] are correct, and print the envelope.

33

Quick Reference

Lesson 1: Previewing and Printing a Document

To display a document in Print Preview

●   On the Standard toolbar, click the Print Preview button.

To change from single-page view to multiple-page view

1   On the Standard toolbar, click the Print Preview button.
2   On the Print Preview toolbar, click the Multiple Pages button and select the number of pages that you want to display.

To magnify text for editing in Print Preview

1   On the Standard toolbar, click the Print Preview button.
2   In the Print Preview window, position the mouse pointer on the document.
3   When the pointer changes to a magnifying glass, click the area of the document that you want to magnify.

To edit text in Print Preview

1   On the Standard toolbar, click Print Preview.
2   On the Print Preview toolbar, click the Magnifier button to turn the magnifying glass into the insertion point.

To insert a page break

1   Click in the document where you want the page to break.
2   On the Insert menu, click Break.
3   In the Break dialog box, click the Page Break option, and then click OK.

To adjust margins using the ruler

1   Place the pointer on the edge of the ruler, where the margin marker is, and wait for the pointer to change into a double-headed arrow.
2   Press Alt and then drag to change the margins.

To print a whole document

●   On the Standard toolbar, click the Print button. Or, on the Print Preview toolbar, click the Print button.

To print part of a document using dialog box options

1   On the File menu, click Print.
2   Select the options you want in the Print dialog box.

■ **Putting It All Together exercises.** These exercises give you another opportunity to practice skills that you learned in the lesson. Completing these exercises helps you to verify whether you understand the lesson, to reinforce your learning, and to retain what you have learned by applying what you have learned in a different way.

■ **Quick Reference.** A complete summary of steps for tasks taught in each lesson is available in the back of the guide. This is often the feature that people find most useful when they return to their workplaces. The expert-level guides include the references from the core-level guides so that you can review or refresh basic and advanced skills on your own whenever necessary.

■ **Index.** Student guides are completely indexed. All glossary terms and application features appear in the index.

Suggestions for Improvements

Microsoft welcomes your feedback on the *Step by Step Courseware* series. Your comments and suggestions will help us to improve future versions of this training product. Please send your feedback to SBSCfdbk@microsoft.com.

Support requests for Microsoft products should not be directed to this alias. Please see "Using the CD-ROM" for information on support contacts.

Conventions and Features Used in This Book

This book uses special fonts, symbols, and heading conventions to highlight important information or to call your attention to special steps. For more information about the features available in each lesson, refer to the "Course Overview" section on page vii.

Convention	Meaning
Sample files for the lesson	This icon identifies the section that lists the files that the lesson will use and explains any file preparation that you need to take care of before starting the lesson.
An ISP that also provides Web hosting services for companies and individuals is sometimes called a Web Presence Provider (WPP).	Notes in the margin area are pointers to information provided elsewhere in the workbook or provide brief notes related to the text or procedures.
New!	This icon indicates a new or greatly improved feature in this version of the software product and includes a short description of what is new.
FP2000.5.1	This icon indicates that the section where this icon appears covers a Microsoft Office User Specialist (MOUS) exam objective. The number below the icon is the MOUS objective number. For a complete list of the MOUS objectives, see the "MOUS Objective List" section on page xxi.
tip	Tips provide helpful hints or alternative procedures related to particular tasks.
important	Importants provide warnings or cautions that are critical to exercises.
Save	When a toolbar button is referenced in the lesson, the button's picture and label are shown in the margin.
Alt+Tab	A plus sign (+) between two key names means that you must press those keys at the same time. For example, "Press Alt+Tab" means that you hold down the Alt key while you press Tab.
Boldface type	This formatting indicates text that you need to type Or It indicates a glossary entry that is defined at the end of the lesson.

Using the CD-ROM

The CD-ROM included with this student guide contains the practice files that you'll use as you perform the exercises in the book. By using the practice files, you won't waste time creating the samples used in the lessons, and you can concentrate on learning how to use Microsoft FrontPage 2000. With the files and the step-by-step instructions in the lessons, you'll also learn by doing, which is an easy and effective way to acquire and remember new skills.

The CD-ROM also includes a Microsoft Word file called Testbank.doc, which provides multiple-choice and true/false questions that you can use to test your knowledge following the completion of each lesson or the completion of the *Microsoft FrontPage 2000 Step by Step Courseware Core Skills* course.

System Requirements

Your computer system must meet the following minimum requirements for you to install the practice files from the CD-ROM and to run Microsoft FrontPage 2000.

> ### important
> The FrontPage 2000 software is not provided on the companion CD-ROM at the back of this book. This course assumes that you have already purchased and installed FrontPage 2000.

- A personal computer running Microsoft FrontPage 2000 on a Pentium 75-megahertz (MHz) or higher processor with the Microsoft Windows 95 or later operating system with 24 MB of RAM, or the Microsoft Windows NT Workstation version 4.0 operating system with Service Pack 3 and 40 MB of RAM.

- Internet access.

- At least 15 MB of available disk space (after installing FrontPage 2000 or Microsoft Office 2000).

- A CD-ROM drive.

- A monitor with VGA or higher resolution (Super VGA recommended; 15-inch monitor or larger recommended).

- A Microsoft mouse, a Microsoft IntelliMouse, or other compatible pointing device.

If You Need to Install
or Uninstall the Practice Files

Your instructor might already have installed the practice files before you arrive in class. However, your instructor might ask you to install the practice files on your own at the start of class. Also, if you want to work through any of the exercises in this workbook on your own at home or at your place of business after class, you will need to first install the practice files.

To install the practice files:

1   Insert the CD-ROM in the CD-ROM drive of your computer.

A menu screen appears. If the menu screen does not appear, double-click StartCD.exe in the root of the CD-ROM.

> ## important
> If the menu screen does not appear, start Windows Explorer. In the left pane, locate the icon for your CD-ROM, and click this icon. In the right pane, double-click the file StartCD.

2   Click the Install Practice Files button, and follow the instructions on the screen.

The setup program window appears with recommended options preselected for you.

3   After the files have been installed, click the Exit option to close the menu, and remove the CD-ROM from your CD-ROM drive.

A folder called FrontPage Core Practice has been created on your hard disk, the practice files have been placed in that folder, and a shortcut to the Microsoft Press Web site has been added to your desktop.

Use the following steps when you want to delete the lesson practice Webs from your hard disk. Your instructor might ask you to perform these steps at the end of class. Also, you will want to perform these steps if you have worked through the exercises at home or at your place of business and want to work through the exercises again. Deleting the practice files and then reinstalling them ensures that all files and folders are in their original condition if you decide to work through the exercises again.

To uninstall the practice files:

1   On the Windows taskbar, click the Start button, point to Settings, and then click Control Panel.

2   Double-click the Add/Remove icon.

3   Click FrontPage Core Practice in the list, and click Change/Remove. (If your computer has Windows 2000 Professional installed, click the Remove button.)

4   Click Yes when the confirmation dialog box appears.

Using the Practice Files

Each lesson in this book explains when and how to use any practice files for that lesson. The lessons are built around scenarios that simulate a real work environment, so you can easily apply the skills you learn to your own work. The scenarios in the lessons use the context of the fictitious Lakewood Mountains Resort, a hotel and convention center located in the mountains of California.

The following is a list of all files and folders used in the lessons. Note that a Web folder might contain more files than are shown here—to support the correct display of a Web and for use with the Putting It All Together sections at the end of each lesson. This list contains only those files that are actually used in the lesson exercises.

File Name	Description
Lesson01 - folder	Folder used in Lesson 1
History.htm	File used in Lesson 1
Welcome.htm	File used in Lesson 1
Bugrep.htm	File used in Lesson 2
Discuss.htm	File used in Lesson 2
HomePage.htm	File used in Lesson 2
Index.htm	File used in Lesson 2
Location.htm	File used in Lesson 2
Recreati.htm	File used in Lesson 2
Work	Folder used in Lesson 2
Lesson03 - folder	Folder used in Lesson 3
FAQ.htm	File used in Lesson 3
Index.htm	File used in Lesson 3
Location.htm	File used in Lesson 3
Main_building.jpg	Image used in Lesson 3
Recreati.htm	File used in Lesson 3
Lesson04 - folder	Folder used in Lesson 4
Reasons.htm	File used in Lesson 4
Welcome.htm	File used in Lesson 4
Lesson05 - folder	Folder used in Lesson 5
Directions_to_ Lakewood.htm	File used in Lesson 5
Location.rtf	File used in Lesson 5
Onthe.htm	File used in Lesson 5
Special_programs_ for_kids.htm	File used in Lesson 5
Lesson06 - folder	Folder used in Lesson 6
Boat_trips.jpg	Image used in Lesson 6
Bry_gap.jpg	Image used in Lesson 6
Dragdrop.avi	Motion clip used in Lesson 6
FrontPageLogo.gif	Image used in Lesson 6
Main_building.jpg	Image used in Lesson 6
Pc_help01.htm	File used in Lesson 6
Pc_help03.htm	File used in Lesson 6
Sights01.htm	File used in Lesson 6
Sights02.htm	File used in Lesson 6
Sights03.htm	File used in Lesson 6
Tolizt01.mid	Sound clip used in Lesson 6

(continued)

continued

File Name	Description
Welcome01.htm	File used in Lesson 6
Welcome02.htm	File used in Lesson 6
Welcome03.htm	File used in Lesson 6
Lesson07 - folder	Folder used in Lesson 7
Dining.htm	File used in Lesson 7
History.htm	File used in Lesson 7
Index.htm	File used in Lesson 7
Location.htm	File used in Lesson 7
Lesson08 - folder	Folder used in Lesson 8
Dhtml01.htm	File used in Lesson 8
Index.htm	File used in Lesson 8
Index01.htm	File used in Lesson 8
Index02.htm	File used in Lesson 8
Index03a.htm	File used in Lesson 8

Replying to Install Messages

When you work through some lessons, you might see a message indicating that the feature that you are trying to use is not installed. If you see this message, insert the Microsoft FrontPage 2000 CD or Microsoft Office 2000 CD 1 in your CD-ROM drive, and click Yes to install the feature.

Locating and Importing Files

After you (or your instructor) have installed the practice files, all the files you need for this course will be stored in a folder named FrontPage Core Practice located on your hard disk. To navigate to this folder from within FrontPage:

1   On the File menu, click Open to display the Open dialog box.

2   Click the Look In down arrow, and click the icon for your hard disk.

3   Double-click the folder named FrontPage Core Practice.

All the folders for the lessons appear within the FrontPage Core Practice folder.

In FrontPage, you can open a selected file or you can create a Web, which is a collection of all files and subfolders for a Web site. When you create a Web, FrontPage creates a new Web folder and creates an index for all files and subfolders in the Web. FrontPage updates this index internally when you create new files, insert pictures, delete files, and rename files.

Although you don't have to know how the index works, it's important to recognize that you cannot simply open an existing folder and use it as a Web. Instead you must first import the folder. When you import a folder in FrontPage, the program creates a new Web folder, places all files from the original folder in this new folder, and creates the index.

At the start of most lessons in this course, you will need to import a folder to create a FrontPage Web so that you can work through the exercises in the lesson. On the first page of each lesson, look for the margin icon *Sample files for the lesson*. This icon points to the paragraph that explains which folder that you will need to import before you can begin the lesson exercises. The first three steps for importing a Web serve as a reminder of the complete steps that you need to perform to import the folder as a new Web.

Use the following complete set of steps whenever you need to import a Web. After you import a Web a few times, you probably won't need to refer to the steps below. You can use the first three steps provided at the start of a lesson to refresh your memory regarding the complete steps to perform. The following steps describe how to import a Web, using the folder for Lesson 3 as an example.

1   On the File menu, point to New, and then click Web.

    FrontPage displays the New dialog box.

2   Click the Import Web Wizard icon.

3   In the Specify The Location Of The New Web box, delete the default text and type **C:\My Webs\Lesson03**, where C is the letter of your hard disk.

4   Click OK to continue.

    FrontPage displays the first Import Web Wizard dialog box.

5   Click the From A Source Directory Of Files option, select the Include Subfolders check box, and click the Browse button.

6   Navigate to the Lesson03 folder in the FrontPage Core Practice folder, and click OK.

7   Click Next twice, and then click Finish.

    FrontPage creates a new Web based on the practice files and places the files in the new Web folder.

If You Need Help with the Practice Files

If you have any problems regarding the use of this book's CD-ROM, you should first consult your instructor. If you are using the CD-ROM at home or at your place of business and need additional help with the practice files, see the Microsoft Press Support Web site at *http://mspress.microsoft.com/support*.

important

Please note that support for the FrontPage 2000 software product itself is not offered through the above Web site. For help using FrontPage 2000, rather than this Microsoft Press book, you can visit *www.microsoft.com/ support* or call FrontPage 2000 Technical Support at (425) 635-7070 on weekdays between 6 A.M. and 6 P.M. Pacific Standard Time. Microsoft Product Support does not provide support for this course.

MOUS Objective List

Taking a Microsoft Office User Specialist Certification Test

The Microsoft Office User Specialist (MOUS) program is the only Microsoft-approved certification program designed to measure and validate your skills with the Microsoft Office suite of desktop productivity applications: Microsoft Word, Microsoft Excel, Microsoft PowerPoint, Microsoft Access, and Microsoft Outlook.

By becoming certified, you demonstrate to employers that you have achieved a predictable level of skills in the use of a particular Office application. Certification is often required by employers either as a condition of employment or as a condition of advancement within the company or other organization. The certification examinations are sponsored by Microsoft but administered through Nivo International.

For each Microsoft Office 2000 application, two levels of MOUS tests are currently or will soon be available: core and expert. For a core-level test, you demonstrate your ability to use an application knowledgeably and without assistance in a day-to-day work environment. For an expert-level test, you demonstrate that you have a thorough knowledge of the application and can effectively apply all or most of the features of the application to solve problems and complete tasks found in business.

Preparing to Take an Exam

Unless you're a very experienced user, you'll need to use a test preparation course to prepare to complete the test correctly and within the time allowed. The *Step by Step Courseware* training program is designed to prepare you for either core-level or expert-level knowledge of a particular Microsoft Office application. By the end of this course, you should have a strong knowledge of all exam topics, and with some additional review and practice on your own, you should feel confident in your ability to pass the appropriate exam.

After you decide which exam to take, review the list of objectives for the exam. This list can be found in the "MOUS Objective List" at the front of the appropriate *Step by Step Courseware* student guide. You can also easily identify tasks that are included in the objective list by locating the MOUS logo in the margin of this book's lessons.

For an expert-level test, you'll need to be able to demonstrate any of the skills from the core-level objective list, too. Expect some of these core-level tasks to appear on the expert-level test. In the *Step by Step Courseware* expert skills student guides, you'll find a task reference that includes the core skills in the "Quick Reference" section at the back of the book.

You can also familiarize yourself with a live MOUS certification test by downloading and installing a MOUS certification test demonstration from *www.mous.net*.

To take the MOUS test, first see *www.mous.net* to locate your nearest testing center. Then call the testing center directly to schedule your test. The amount of advance notice you should provide will vary for different testing centers, and it typically depends on the number of computers available at the testing center, the number of other testers who have already been scheduled for the day on which you want to take the test, and the number of times per week that the testing center offers MOUS testing. In general, you should call to schedule your test at least two weeks prior to the date on which you want to take the test.

When you arrive at the testing center, you might be asked for proof of identity. A driver's license or passport is an acceptable form of identification. If you do not have either of these items of documentation, call your testing center and ask what alternative forms of identification will be accepted. If you are retaking a test, bring your MOUS identification number, which will have been given to you when you previously took the test. If you have not prepaid or if your organization has not already arranged to make payment for you, you will need to pay the test-taking fee when you arrive. The current test-taking fee is $50 (U.S.).

Test Format

All MOUS certification tests are live, performance-based tests. There are no multiple-choice, true/false, or short answer questions. Instructions are general: you are told the basic tasks to perform on the computer, but you aren't given any help in figuring out how to perform them. You are not permitted to use reference material other than the application's online Help system.

As you complete the tasks stated in a particular test question, the testing software monitors your actions. An example question might be:

> Open the Web paged named *AboutUs*. Select the text *Our San Diego Office*, and create a hyperlink to the Web paged named *SanDiego*. Create the hyperlink so that it is displayed with a blinking effect. Save the *SanDiego* Web page and then preview it in your Web browser.

The sample tests available from *www.mous.net* give you a clear idea of the type of questions that you will be asked on the actual test.

When the test administrator seats you at a computer, you'll see an online form that you use to enter information about yourself (name, address, and other information required to process your exam results). When you complete the form, the software will take a few minutes to generate the test from a master test bank and will then prompt you to continue. The first test question will appear in a window. Read the question carefully, and then perform all the tasks stated in the test question. When you have finished completing all tasks for a question, click the Next Question button.

You have 45 to 60 minutes to complete all questions, depending on the test that you are taking. The testing software assesses your results as soon as you complete the test, and the results of the test can be printed by the test administrator so that you will have a record of any tasks that you performed incorrectly. A passing grade is 75 percent or higher. If you pass, you will receive a certificate in the mail within two to four weeks. If you do not pass, you can study and practice the skills that you missed and then schedule to retake the test at a later date.

Tips for Successfully Completing the Test

The following tips and suggestions are the result of feedback received by many individuals who have taken one or more MOUS tests:

- Make sure that you are thoroughly prepared. If you have extensively used the application for which you are being tested, you might feel confident that you are prepared for the test. However, the test might include questions that involve tasks that you rarely or never perform when you use the application at your place of business, at school, or at home. You must be knowledgeable in *all* the MOUS objectives for the test that you will take.

- Read each exam question carefully. An exam question might include several tasks that you are to perform. A partially correct response to a test question is counted as an incorrect response. In the example question provided on the previous page, you might open the correct Web page, select the correct text, and create the hyperlink, but neglect to define the hyperlink so that it blinks. This would count as an incorrect response and would result in a lower test score.

- You are allowed to use the application's online Help system, but relying on online Help too much will slow you down and possibly prevent you from completing the test within the allotted time. Use online Help only when necessary.

- Keep track of your time. The test does not display the amount of time that you have left, so you need to keep track of the time yourself by monitoring your start time and the required end time on your watch or a clock in the testing center (if there is one). The test program displays the number of items that you have completed along with the total number of test items (for instance, "35 of 40 items have been completed"). Use this information to gauge your pace.

- If you skip a question, you cannot return to it later. You should skip a question only if you are certain that you cannot complete the tasks correctly.

- Don't worry if the testing software crashes while you are taking the exam. The test software is set up to handle this situation. Find your test administrator and tell him or her what happened. The administrator will work through the steps required to restart the test. When the test restarts, it will allow you to continue where you left off. You will have the same amount of time remaining to complete the test as you did when the software crashed.

- As soon as you are finished reading a question and you click in the application window, a condensed version of the instruction is displayed in a corner of the screen. If you are unsure whether you have completed all tasks stated in the test question, click the Instructions button on the test information bar at the bottom of the screen and then reread the question. Close the instruction window when you are finished. Do this as often as necessary to ensure you have read the question correctly and that you have completed all the tasks stated in the question.

If You Do Not Pass the Test

If you do not pass, you can use the assessment printout as a guide to practice the items that you missed. There is no limit to the number of times that you can retake a test; however, you must pay the fee each time that you take the test. Expect to see some of the same test items on a subsequent test; the test software randomly generates the test items from a master test bank before you begin the test. Also expect to see several questions that did not appear on the previous test.

LESSON 1

Planning a Web Site

After completing this lesson, you will be able to:

✔ *Explain basic Web site structure.*

✔ *Create and import a Web.*

✔ *Use FrontPage views to examine a Web.*

✔ *Close and reopen a Web.*

✔ *Get ideas for a Web site.*

In this lesson, you will learn how Microsoft FrontPage makes it easy for you to create and maintain Web pages and Web sites. FrontPage is more than just a Web site design program; it is also a powerful organizational tool. When you create or import a Web, FrontPage automatically organizes and updates all the files in the Web. Once you start FrontPage, you'll learn how to create a new Web. You will then explore the different ways you can view a Web. FrontPage views are a helpful way to understand the organization of a Web site. When you are finished exploring, you will learn how to close and reopen a Web, and you will quit FrontPage.

Sample files for the lesson

To complete the procedures in this lesson, you will need to create a new Web based on the files in the Lesson01 folder in the FrontPage Core Practice folder that is located on your hard disk.

Understanding FrontPage Webs

The key to creating Web pages is **HTML** (Hypertext Markup Language). HTML uses codes, called **tags**, to format text on a Web page. The Web **browser** that you use (such as Microsoft Internet Explorer) translates these codes into the Web page text and graphics that you see on your screen.

important

In this book (and elsewhere), you'll see the word *Web* used in two different ways. Usually, *Web* refers to the **World Wide Web**. However, it can also refer to a *FrontPage-based Web*, a set of Web pages you create in FrontPage. The context should make it clear what *Web* means in each particular case.

A Web or **Web site** is a collection of related Web pages and other files, such as graphics or sounds. Web sites usually have a specific purpose, whether it is personal or business-related. FrontPage also comes with **wizards**, which walk you step by step through the process of creating a Web site, and **templates**, which are ready-made Web pages containing all of the formatting required to build and customize your own Web pages.

Wizards and templates can help you create several different kinds of Web sites.

On each Web site, one page is designated as the **home page.** This is usually the first page that visitors see when they visit the Web site. On the home page, visitors can click **hyperlinks** to view other pages on the Web site or pages on different Web sites. For instance, a hyperlink might connect to a Web page on the same computer as the first Web site or to a page stored on a computer halfway around the world. Wherever the page, hyperlinks allow you to easily navigate among all the pages in a Web with just a click. A typical Web site organization is shown in the following illustration.

The term *home page* is also used to refer to the first Web page that appears when you start a Web browser. So each Web site has a home page, and your browser has its own home page.

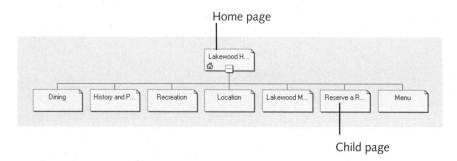

The home page is at the top, with linked pages on the row below it. Usually, each page under the home page—called a **child page** of the home page—contains hyperlinks to the other pages on the Web site, as well as a hyperlink back to the home page so that it's easy for visitors to get around the entire Web site. Often, child pages will have hyperlinks to pages that are below them in the organization, and so forth.

tip

The lessons in this book teach you how to create Web sites for the World Wide Web. You can use the same techniques to create Web sites for an **intranet**— a network that works like the World Wide Web, but has security features so that only people within the company or organization can access its pages.

A Web site resides on a **Web server,** a computer dedicated to making Web pages available to people who want to visit the site. (However, with FrontPage, you can create a Web site right on your computer's hard disk and publish the Web site to a server when you are ready.) Normally a Web server is connected to the **Internet,** which makes its Web pages available for viewing on the World Wide Web. Many companies and organizations set up Web servers on intranets. These private Web servers are ideal for hosting Web sites that contain project files and other internal data that need to be shared by staff members. Some pages of an intranet Web site might be made available to the world, while other pages would remain accessible only to users within the organization. An intranet that provides limited access to visitors outside of an organization is called an **extranet.**

Finding a Service Provider

Before you set up the Web site for your client, Lakewood Mountains Resort, you need to identify a computer that will store the Web files. This computer is called a Web server or a **Web host**.

Most Internet service providers (ISPs) offer Web hosting as part of the package when you buy an Internet account. Web hosting simply means that the ISP provides space on a Web server for your Web files. Online services such as America Online also offer Web hosting. For simple Webs, an ISP's Web hosting services are often adequate. For larger and more sophisticated Webs, such as business or corporate Webs, an account with a dedicated Web host can be a good investment. A dedicated Web host can offer more disk space for your Web files and, often, faster equipment.

Whether you choose an Internet service provider or a dedicated Web host, there's an important question you should always ask: "Do you have the FrontPage Server Extensions?" FrontPage has many extra features to help you create exciting Web sites and put them on the Web with minimal effort. However, some ISPs and Web hosts do not have these FrontPage Server Extensions. Some ISPs provide them for business Internet accounts, but not for the less-expensive personal accounts.

So, where can you find a FrontPage-supporting Web host? On the Web, of course. Navigate to Microsoft's Web Presence Provider site at *www.microsoftwpp.com/wppsearch/* to view lists of ISPs and Web hosts that have the FrontPage Server Extensions installed.

An ISP that also provides Web hosting services for companies and individuals is sometimes called a Web Presence Provider (WPP).

Appendix B, "Internet Service Providers that Support FrontPage," contains a list of Web Presence Providers in the United States and Canada.

Assume you've found a Web host that has the FrontPage Server Extensions. Now you need to decide what should go into the Web site you present to your client. You must first decide on the purpose of the Web site. In the case of Lakewood Mountains Resort, there are two main purposes:

- To provide information about the resort for prospective customers.
- To enable customers to request room reservations over the Web.

Of course, Web sites can have many additional purposes. One Web site might provide technical support for a computer product. Another might have a catalog and allow customers to place secure orders over the Web. The purpose of a Web site determines its design and the pages it should include.

Like all Web sites, the resort's Web site will start with a home page. It then needs at least one page about each of the resort's major selling points. So that customers can request reservations over the Web, the site will also need a form on which customers can enter their name, address, and reservation data.

You call the resort manager to learn about the resort's major selling points. You end up with a list of topics, each of which will get its own Web page:

- The resort's secluded location.
- The resort's recreational facilities.
- The resort's fine food.
- The picturesque town just a few minutes away.
- The resort's colorful history and helpful staff.
- Room reservations.

Based on this information, you come up with a diagram of the Web site.

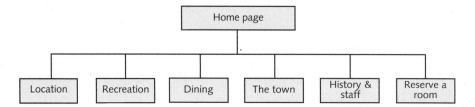

Creating and Importing Webs

There are essentially two ways to create a Web. The first way is to create the Web's pages and other files after you create the Web itself. The second way is to create a new Web based on existing files.

The second approach works especially well when you have a previous version of a Web—whether on your local hard disk or on a remote Web server—and you want to create a new version of it.

The Import Web Wizard creates a new Web site based on existing Web files on your own computer or on a Web server. You can then modify the Web pages and Web structure as needed. You'll find this wizard especially useful for creating and testing updated versions of your own Web sites.

In this exercise, you create a new Web based on the files in the Lesson01 folder in the FrontPage Core Practice folder.

1   On the Windows taskbar, click the Start button, point to Programs, and then click Microsoft FrontPage.

FrontPage starts.

You can also create a desktop shorcut for FrontPage. To create a shortcut, click the Start button, point to Programs, right-click Microsoft FrontPage, point to Send To, and then click Desktop (Create Shortcut).

2   On the File menu, point to New, and click Web.

FrontPage displays the New dialog box.

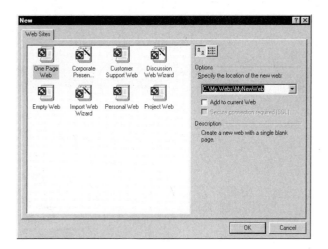

If your hard disk uses a letter other than C, substitute the appropriate drive letter in place of C.

3   Click the Import Web Wizard icon. In the Specify The Location Of The New Web text box, delete the default text, and type **C:\My Webs\Lesson01**, and click OK.

FrontPage displays the first Import Web Wizard dialog box.

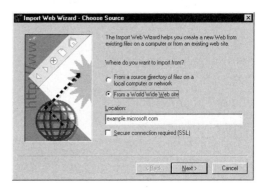

4   Click the From A Source Directory Of Files option, select the Include Subfolders check box, and then click the Browse button.

5   Browse to the Lesson01 folder in the FrontPage Core Practice folder on your hard disk, and click OK.

6   Click Next twice, and click Finish.

FrontPage creates a new Web based on the practice files and places it in the Lesson01 folder.

FP2000.5.1
FP2000.11.1

Exploring FrontPage Views

FrontPage makes it easy not only to create Web pages and Web sites, but also to manage them. The FrontPage window is divided into three main sections (as shown on the following page), each of which gives you a different kind of control over a Web.

Views bar   Folder List   Viewing area

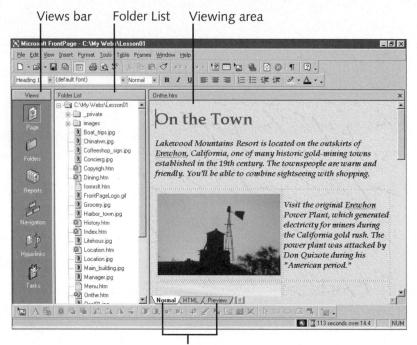

Tabs let you view and edit the
currently selected file in different ways.

In FrontPage, you can view a Web in several different ways. The Views bar
displays icons that let you view and edit different components of
a Web, such as the structure of the Web or the hyperlinks in the Web.
For managing your Web site, the Views bar provides an easy way to
switch between views of your Web structure and pages, including a
new Reports view.

2000 New!

The Views bar now provides an easy
way to switch between views of Web
structure and pages, and it includes
an all-new Reports view.

Icon	View	Description
	Page	Displays a Web page for viewing or editing.
	Folders	Displays a list of folders and files in the current Web.
	Reports	Displays a list of reports on different aspects of the current Web, such as the number of linked files, broken links, and "slow" pages that would take more than 30 seconds to download to a computer over a 28.8-KBps connection. (Thirty seconds is the default value, but it can be changed by the user.)
	Navigation	Displays a tree diagram of the current Web.
	Hyperlinks	Displays a diagram of hyperlinks to and from the current page.

(continued)

continued

Icon	View	Description
	Tasks	Displays a list of tasks to be performed on the current Web. When you use some of the wizards to create a Web, FrontPage compiles a task list. You can also add tasks on your own.

The Folder List displays all folders and files in the current Web, while the currently selected page is displayed in Page view. At the bottom of the screen, a status bar displays information about the current page or operation. When a page is displayed in Page view, for example, the status bar shows an estimated download time for the page over a 28.8-KBps modem connection.

In this exercise, you explore the different views of the new Web.

1   In the Folder List, scroll down, and double-click the file Welcome.htm.

FrontPage displays the Welcome Web page.

> A FrontPage Web includes HTML files and all graphic and multimedia files that appear on Web pages.

Hotel graphic

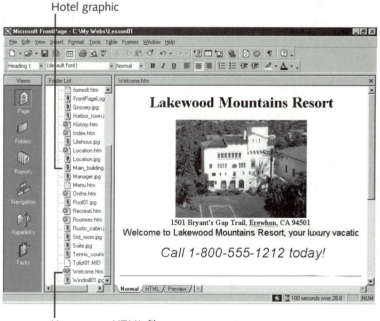

Home page HTML file

2   At the bottom of the FrontPage window, click the HTML tab.

FrontPage displays the HTML code for the current page.

3   At the bottom of the FrontPage window, click the Preview tab.

FrontPage displays a preview of how the page will look in a Web browser. Notice that unlike the marquee that is displayed in Normal view, the scrolling marquee actually scrolls in Preview view.

4   On the Views bar, click the Folders icon.

FrontPage displays a list of all folders and files in the current Web.

Folders view provides a way for you to see detailed information about each file, including the size of the file, the file's extension, and the date on which the file was most recently modified.

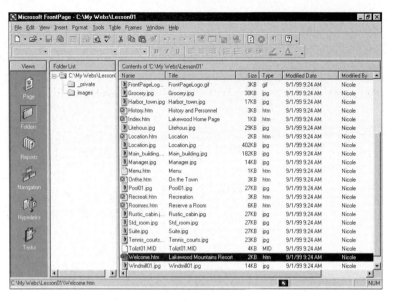

5   On the Views bar, click the Reports icon.

FrontPage displays a list of reports about the current Web.

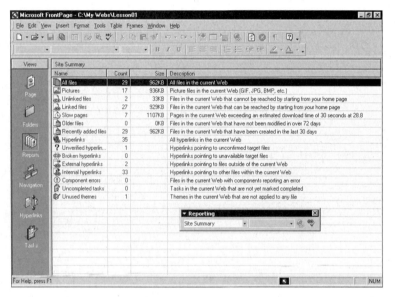

6   On the Views bar, click the Navigation icon.

The Web appears in Navigation view.

FrontPage normally displays a tree diagram of the current Web. However, because you haven't yet created any Web pages, only the home page (Index.htm) appears in Navigation view.

7   On the Views bar, click the Hyperlinks icon, and click the file Welcome.htm in the Folder List. FrontPage displays a diagram of hyperlinks going to and from the page.

The viewing area shows that the Index page contains hyperlinks to the Menu and Welcome Web pages.

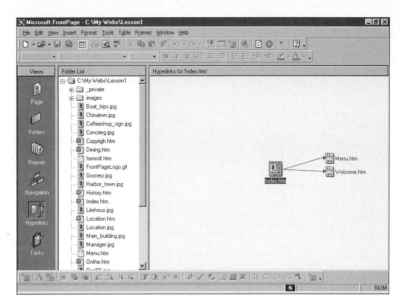

8   On the Views bar, click the Tasks icon.

Currently, there are no tasks to display.

Understanding FrontPage Folders

When you install FrontPage 2000, it creates a folder called My Webs. This is the default folder in which FrontPage will store any Webs you create. Each separate Web you create gets its own subfolder in the My Webs folder. FrontPage uses each of these subfolders to store files specific to that Web.

When FrontPage creates a Web, it also creates at least three different folders in which to store Web pages and files. You don't have to worry about these folders; you can ignore them and your Web will still work perfectly. However, understanding how FrontPage uses these folders can help you organize your files.

Folder	Explanation
main folder	The default folder that FrontPage uses for storing Web pages, images, and Java class files. FrontPage creates this folder within the My Webs folder on your hard disk. You determine the name for the main folder when you name the Web.
_private	FrontPage stores form results in this folder. You can also use this folder to create subfolders that contain files that can be viewed by other Web developers in your team but cannot be viewed by visitors to the Web site.
images	The folder into which you can move image files, if desired. If you have a large number of image files, this folder helps remove clutter from the main folder.

(continued)

continued

Understanding FrontPage Folders

In addition to the three default folders, you can also create your own folders to hold specific types or groups of files.

1   On the Views bar, click the Folders icon.

2   On the File menu, point to New, and click Folder.

FrontPage creates a new folder. The default folder name is New Folder.

3   Delete the default folder name, type the desired name, and then press Enter.

FrontPage renames the folder.

You can create a new folder for any purpose. The only thing you must remember is to use FrontPage—not Windows Explorer—to move files into the folder. When you use FrontPage to move files, any hyperlinks to those files are automatically updated.

FP2000.2.1

Closing and Reopening a Web

Although a Web can actually be dozens or even hundreds of files, FrontPage organizes these files for you—in folders. Each Web is given a name, regardless of how many individual files make up the Web. With this approach, you don't have to remember the names and locations of all the files that form the Web. Instead, you simply use the Web name to instruct FrontPage to open or close the Web.

In this exercise, you close and reopen the Lesson01 Web.

1   On the Views bar, click the Page icon.

The Welcome page is displayed in Preview view.

2   Click the Close button in the top-right corner of the Web page, *not* the Close button in the top-right corner of the FrontPage window.

The Welcome page closes.

3   On the File menu, click Close Web.

FrontPage closes the Lesson01 Web.

4   On the File menu, click Open Web.

FrontPage displays the Open Web dialog box.

When you click Open Web on the File menu, FrontPage displays the contents of the folder you last opened in the Open Web dialog box. However, you can use the Look In down arrow to navigate to any folder on your hard disk or on a network drive.

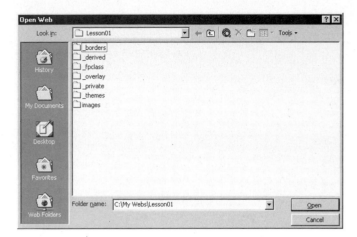

You can also quickly reopen previously created Webs by pointing to Recent Webs on the File menu and clicking the Web you want to reopen.

5 Click the Open button.

FrontPage opens the previously used Web.

6 In the Folder List, double-click the file History.htm.

FrontPage displays the History and Personnel Web page.

Getting Ideas for a Web Site

The best place to find ideas for your Web site is the Internet. The first and most obvious place to look is Microsoft's own FrontPage Web site at *www.microsoft.com/frontpage*. Another place to look is CNet's Builder.com Web site at *www.builder.com*. This site has tutorials on Web design, HTML, scripting, and many other Web topics.

Before you begin planning your own Web, you should explore the World Wide Web to view many different pages and designs. Ideas are everywhere, and as long as you don't just copy the content of someone's Web site, the ideas are free. For example, if you're stuck on how to brighten a boring design, look for other Web sites with designs that appeal to you. Use the Web sites you like as blueprints for improving your design.

In this exercise, you visit Web pages on the Internet to familiarize yourself with some of the sites that offer ideas on Web design.

1 Start your default Web browser.

The Web browser opens and displays your Internet home page.

tip
Take note of at least two design or art elements on each of the Web sites that you visit in this exercise. Think about how you might use the elements in a Web site of your own.

If the End User License Agreement (EULA) is displayed, read the license agreement, and click the Accept button. The EULA appears only the first time you visit the Web site on a particular computer.

2 In the Address bar, type **www.microsoft.com/clipgallerylive**, and press Enter.

The End User License Agreement (EULA) appears.

Microsoft's Clip Gallery Live Web page is continuously updated. When you visit the page on the Web, it will look different from the figure shown here.

3 Read the license agreement if it appears, and click the Accept button.

The Microsoft ClipGallery Live Web page appears in your browser. From here you can download clip art, photo images, sounds, and videos.

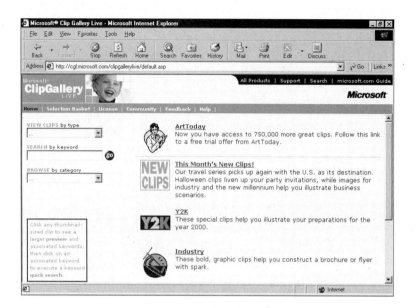

4 In the Address bar, type **www.microsoft.com/frontpage**, and press Enter.

Microsoft's FrontPage home page appears in your browser.

5 In the Address bar, type **www.builder.com**, and press Enter.

The CNet Builder.com Web page appears in your browser.

Lesson Wrap-Up

This lesson covered how to create and import Webs, how to view a Web using different FrontPage views, how to close and reopen a Web, and how to get ideas for a Web site by browsing the Internet.

If you are continuing to the next lesson:

Close

1 Click the Close button in the top-right corner of your Web browser.

Your Web browser closes, and FrontPage appears.

2 On the File menu, click Close Web. If FrontPage prompts you to save changes, click Yes.

FrontPage saves any changes, and closes the Lesson 01 Web.

If you are not continuing to other lessons:

Close

● Click the Close button in the top-right corner of the FrontPage window. If FrontPage prompts you to save changes, click Yes.

FrontPage saves any changes, closes the Web, and then exits.

Lesson Glossary

browser A program, such as Microsoft Internet Explorer, that uses the Hypertext Transfer Protocol (HTTP) to display the text, graphics, and other multimedia content of a Web site.

child page A page that is organized as a link one level below the page on which the link appears.

extranet An intranet that uses World Wide Web technology to provide access to visitors outside the organization.

home page Typically, the first page that visitors see when they visit a Web site. From the home page, visitors can click hyperlinks to jump to other pages on the Web site or to pages on different Web sites.

HTML Acronym for *Hypertext Markup Language*, which is a standardized tagging method for defining formatting, hyperlinks, and other special handling of text, images, and objects on a Web page to indicate how a browser should display the page.

hyperlinks Text or graphic items on a Web page that, when clicked, cause the Web browser to display a different Web page or Web site.

Internet A worldwide system of computer networks that uses a common set of protocols to transfer information. It commonly supports services such as e-mail, the World Wide Web, and file transfer.

intranet A network that works like the World Wide Web but has security features so that only users within the company or organization can access its pages.

tags Embedded HTML codes that specify formatting for text and graphics for proper display in a Web browser.

templates Ready-made Web pages containing all the formatting required to build a page.

Web host Any computer connected directly to the World Wide Web that acts as a repository for Web site services, stores Web sites, and is available to other computers on the Web. Also called a *Web server*.

Web site A group of HTML documents and associated files that covers one or more related topics and is interconnected by hyperlinks on the World Wide Web.

Web server See *Web host*.

wizards Interactive utilities designed to guide you through the steps for completing a particular task.

World Wide Web The collection of billions of files, stored on computers throughout the world, that contains the content viewable in most Web browsers.

Quick Quiz

1   A(n) _____ _____ is where you store a Web site so that it's available on the Internet.

2   What is the first step in planning a Web?

3   How do you open a Web in FrontPage?

4   How do you change the view of a Web in FrontPage?

5   How do you close a Web in FrontPage?

Putting It All Together

Exercise 1: Open the Lesson01 Web. Use FrontPage views to find the Grocery.jpg file. Then find the Web page where the picture is located and display the HTML formatting of the picture.

Exercise 2: As you plan the Lakewood Mountains Resort Web site, your colleague needs some preliminary information on how much disk space the Web site will require on a Web server. To find this information, view the available reports in the Lesson01 Web, and find the best report type for giving your colleague these preliminary statistics.

LESSON 2

Creating a Web Site

After completing this lesson, you will be able to:

✔ *Create a Web.*

✔ *Create a new page.*

✔ *Add and format Web page text.*

✔ *Change Web page properties.*

✔ *Preview a Web page.*

✔ *Organize a Web.*

✔ *View and print a Web structure.*

Now that you've identified the purposes of a Web site and understand which pages it should include, it's time to start creating a Web with Microsoft FrontPage.

In this lesson, you will learn about FrontPage tools that can help you create a Web site in record time. You will create a Web, add several Web pages, and then preview the way the pages will look by viewing the pages in your default browser. You will also perform other basic Web creation tasks, including organizing pages into a hierarchy, printing a Web, finding text on a Web, and importing files into a Web from a different Web or folder location.

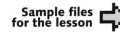
Sample files for the lesson

You will not need any sample files for this lesson. Instead, you will create all of the files and folders needed during the course of this lesson.

FP2000.1.1
FP2000.1.2

Creating a Web Using a Wizard

You can create a Web in FrontPage in three ways: use a wizard, use a template, or create the Web "from scratch." The method you choose depends on your specific needs and situation. Unless you have a lot of experience creating Web sites, you'll probably want to use a template or a wizard to help you create a Web. A FrontPage **template** is a ready-made Web site that you can modify for your needs. Use a template when you want to create a Web quickly.

FrontPage wizards are best used for complex Web sites. Each **wizard** creates a different type of Web using a series of dialog boxes in which you select the specific options that fit your situation.

After you've made all your selections, the wizard creates the Web based on your input. FrontPage includes the following wizards:

This Wizard	Creates
Corporate Presence	A Web for a company. The Web includes a home page, a table of contents, a What's New page, a News Release page, a product and service directory, a Web page for each product or service, a Customer Feedback page, and a Web page that lets visitors search the site.
Customer Support	A Web in which a company can answer customer questions and get feedback. It combines a message board with several other features, such as a frequently asked questions list (FAQ), a suggestion form, and an area for downloading information and software.
Discussion	A Web with a message board. It allows visitors to view, post, and reply to messages on a Web site.
Import	A Web from files stored in a folder on your hard disk or on a network, or from a site that's already on the Internet.

In this exercise, you create a Web using the Corporate Presence Wizard.

1   On the File menu, point to New, and click Web.

FrontPage displays the New dialog box.

You can easily identify a wizard in FrontPage or any Microsoft office application because its icon always contains a "magic wand." One Page Web, Empty Web, Personal Web, and Project Web are templates, not wizards. Templates are explained later in this lesson.

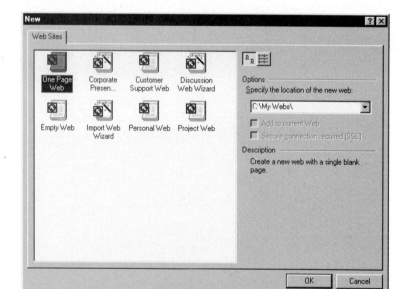

2   Click the Corporate Presence Wizard icon. In the Specify The Location Of The New Web box, delete the default text, and type **C:\My Webs\MyWizardDemo**, and click OK.

If your hard disk uses a letter other than C, substitute the appropriate drive letter in place of C.

FrontPage displays the first Corporate Presence Web Wizard dialog box, which explains the purpose of the Corporate Web Wizard.

3   Click Next.

FrontPage displays the second Corporate Presence Web Wizard dialog box in which you can select pages to include in the Web.

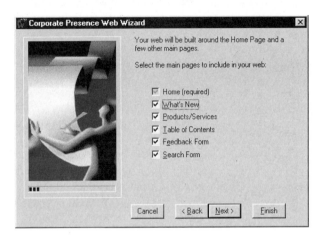

4   Clear the What's New check box and the Search Form check box, and click Next.

FrontPage will not include a What's New or a Search Form page in the Web. The wizard displays the next dialog box in which you select the information to be displayed on the corporate home page.

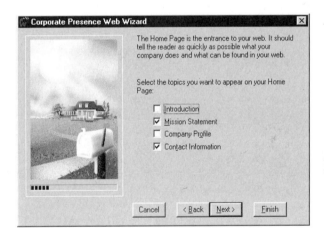

5   Select the Introduction check box, and click Next.

FrontPage will display an introduction section on the corporate presence home page.

The wizard displays the next dialog box in which you select how many pages the wizard should create to show information about products and services.

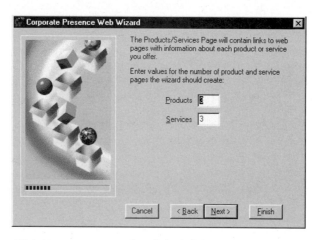

6   Click Next to accept the default of three products pages and three services pages.

The wizard displays a dialog box in which you can select the information that you want displayed on each product or service Web page.

Select the product image check box if you want to include a placeholder for a picture of each product. You can insert these pictures later.

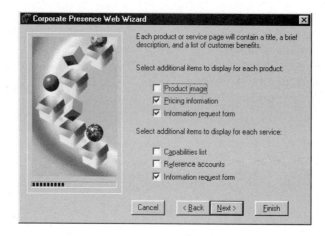

Notice that the Mailing Address check box is not selected. It's standard Web etiquette to request an e-mail address, but not the visitor's mailing address.

7 Click Next to accept the defaults.

FrontPage displays a dialog box in which you can select the information that you want to collect from Web site visitors who fill out the Feedback Form.

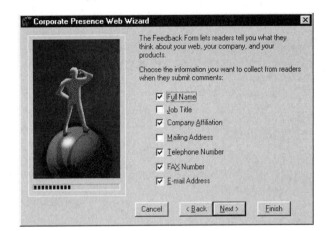

8 Click Next five times.

FrontPage displays a dialog box in which you enter the company name and address.

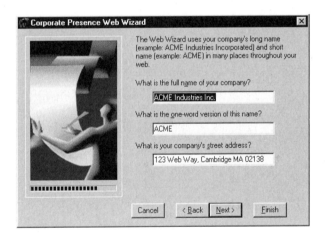

important

In steps 9 and 10, make sure you use the Tab key to move to the next box. If you press Enter, FrontPage will display the next wizard dialog box.

9 In the What Is The Full Name Of Your Company? box, type **Lakewood Mountains Resort**, and press Tab.

10 In the second box, type **LMR**, and press Tab.

11 In the final box, type **1501 Bryant's Gap Trail, Erewhon, CA 94501**, and click Finish.

FrontPage creates a corporate presence Web based on the options that you selected and the information that you entered. FrontPage then displays a list of additional tasks that you need to perform to complete the Web.

12   On the Views bar, click the Navigation icon, and in Navigation view, double-click the home page icon.

FrontPage displays the corporate presence home page. You can now modify the page by entering additional information.

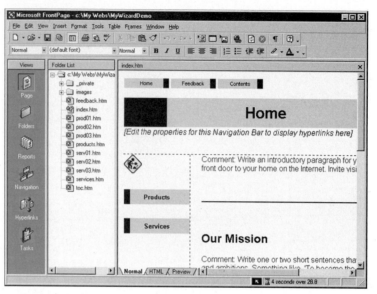

You can also display the home page by double-clicking Index.htm in the Folder List. The home page for a Web is usually named either Index or Default.

13   On the File menu, click Close Web.

FrontPage closes the corporate presence Web.

tip

Get into the habit of creating Web file names that do not contain spaces. Most Web servers do not recognize spaces in file names. If you want to keep the Web file names descriptive, you can separate words and still keep them connected by placing the underscore character (_) between words. For instance, use Recreation_and_services.htm.

FP2000.1.3

Creating a Web Using a Template

Unlike wizards, which prompt you for information and then design a Web based on that input, templates are ready-made Web sites or Web pages that you can modify for your own needs. FrontPage includes the following templates for Webs.

This Template	Creates
Customer Support	A Web site in which a company can answer customer questions and get feedback. It combines a message board with several other features, such as a frequently asked questions list (FAQ), a suggestion form, and an area for downloading information and software.

(continued)

continued

This Template	Creates
Project Web	A Web site to share information about a project with members of a project team. It includes a page that lists team members, a schedule page, a project status page, a message board, and a search page.
Personal Web	A Web site to showcase the interests of an individual. It includes a home page, a photo album page, an interests page, and a Web page for links to other Web sites.
One Page Web	A Web site with only a home page. You might want to use this template as a starting point, adding other pages as you work.
Empty Web	A Web site that you build from scratch. FrontPage creates folders for the site but does not include any Web pages.

In this exercise, you create a Web using the Customer Support Web template.

1   On the File menu, point to New, and click Web.

FrontPage displays the New dialog box.

2   Click the Customer Support Web icon.

FrontPage will use the Customer Support Web template. This template creates a Web site designed to provide help and solve problems for visitors who use a company's products.

3   In the Specify The Location Of The New Web box, delete the default text, type **C:\My Webs\MyTempDemo**, and then click OK.

FrontPage creates a new Web based on the Customer Support Web template.

4   In the Folder List, double-click the file Index.htm.

FrontPage displays the new Web's home page.

> If your hard disk uses a letter other than C, substitute the appropriate drive letter in place of C.

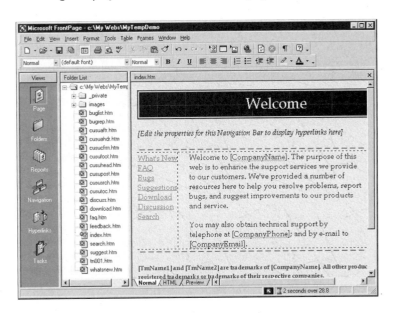

5   Select the text *[CompanyName]*, and type **Lakewood Mountains Software**.

FrontPage replaces the selected text with the text that you typed.

Save

6   On the Standard toolbar, click the Save button.

FrontPage saves the Web page with your changes.

7   In the Folder List, double-click the file Bugrep.htm.

FrontPage displays the Web page that customers can use to report problems with the company's products or services.

8   In the Folder List, double-click the file Discuss.htm.

FrontPage displays a Web page that allows users to read and respond to messages in a discussion board.

9   On the File menu, click Close Web.

FrontPage closes the Customer Support Web.

10   On the File menu, point to New, and click Web.

FrontPage displays the New dialog box.

11   Click the Empty Web icon.

FrontPage will create folders for the Web but will not create any Web pages.

If your hard disk uses a letter other than C, substitute the appropriate drive letter in place of C.

12   In the Specify The Location Of The New Web box, delete the default text, type **C:\My Webs\LakewoodDemo**, and then click OK.

FrontPage creates a new empty Web. You will use this Web for the remainder of the lesson.

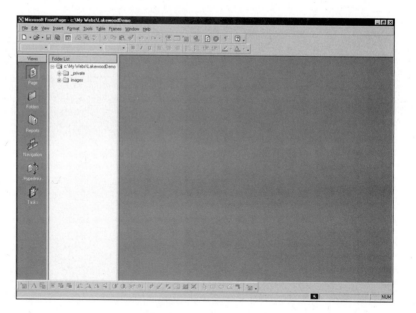

If you already have a Web open, and you want to create a page template, the page will be added to the current Web.

Page Templates

FrontPage also includes templates that you can use to add individual pages, rather than a complete Web. To use a template to create a page, click the Page icon on the Views bar. On the File menu, point to New, and click Page. FrontPage displays the New dialog box with a list of page templates. Click the icon for the type of page that you want to create, and click OK. The following page templates are also used by the Corporate Presence Wizard to create a complete Web.

Template Name	Explanation
Home	A home page containing information that you specify.
What's New	A page with information about new pages or other updates on the Web site.
Products/Services	One or more pages about products or services offered by a company, with a description of each product or service, benefits, part numbers, and pricing.
Table of Contents	Lists all the pages in the Web site, with a hyperlink to each page.
Feedback Form	Allows Web site visitors to send feedback to an e-mail address that you specify.
Search Form	Allows Web site visitors to search the Web site for pages containing words that they specify.

FP2000.4.1
FP2000.4.2

Creating a New Web Page in Page View

A Web can have just a single Web page. For a personal Web, you might consider this option. But the Lakewood Mountains Resort Web needs several pages. You'll find that with FrontPage, adding pages is easy to do.

To add a page, you can either create a new page or import an existing page. If you choose to create a new page, you can do so in most views. If you create a new page with the Web displayed in Navigation view (the view displayed when you click the Navigation icon on the Views bar), FrontPage creates a blank page and adds it to the Web.

There's an advantage to creating a page while the Web is shown in Page view (the view displayed when you click the Page icon on the Views bar). If you create a page in this view, you can use FrontPage's Web page wizards and templates. If you create a page in other views, FrontPage creates a new blank page.

Templates include placeholder text, which provides instructions that you use to replace the placeholder text with "real" text that is relevant to your Web page. In this illustration, all of the text in the Comment Guest Book paragraph represents place-holder text.

Just like the templates for a Web, the templates for Web *pages* are predesigned Web page blueprints for specific purposes. When you create a page with the Guest Book template, for example, the new page contains features and layout needed for a Web site guest book. As shown in the figure below, you simply add your own text, and the page is ready to use.

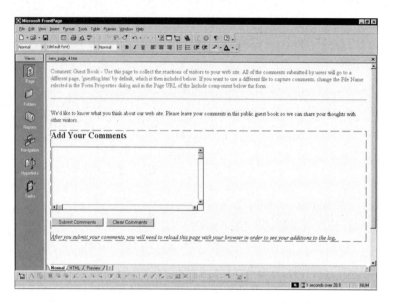

The Web page title is the text that is displayed in the title bar of most Web browsers. You can modify the Web page title without changing the page's file name.

When you create the Web for Lakewood Mountains Resort, you'll create new pages in both Navigation and Page view, and you'll import an existing page. After you've created a Web, the next step is to add Web pages. By default, the first page you add will be treated as the Web's home page. The default file name for the home page is either Default.htm or Index.htm, although the Web page title can be anything you choose.

In this exercise, you create a home page for Lakewood Mountains Resort. You then view the list of page templates that FrontPage provides. Finally, you create the page using the Normal (blank page) template.

You must follow step 1 if you want to display a list of page templates. If you click the New Page button on the Standard toolbar, FrontPage will create a new, blank Web page; you will not have an opportunity to select a page template.

1   On the File menu, point to New, and click Page.

FrontPage displays the New dialog box, which contains templates and wizards for individual pages.

You can click the Details button (the second button above the Options check boxes) to view the complete name of each template.

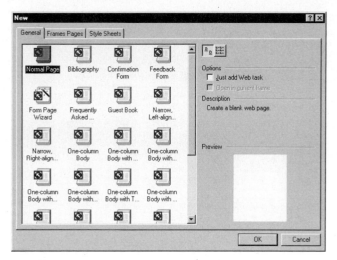

2 Click the icon for the Narrow, Left-Aligned Body template.

FrontPage displays the Web page layout in the Preview section.

3 Scroll down, and click the icon for the Three-Column Body template.

FrontPage displays the Web page layout in the Preview section.

4 Click the Frames Pages tab at the top of the dialog box.

FrontPage displays available templates for frames pages.

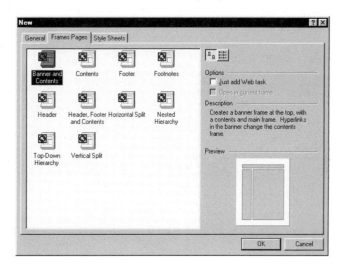

5 Click the General tab, click the icon for the Normal Page template, and then click OK.

FrontPage creates a new, blank Web page and displays it in Page view.

Save

6 On the Standard toolbar, click the Save button.

FrontPage displays the Save As dialog box.

7   Type **HomePage**, and click Save.

FrontPage saves the page using the name you've provided and adds the name of the page to the Folder List.

New Page

> # tip
> You can also create a new page by clicking the New Page button at the left end of the Standard toolbar. Click the down arrow to view all the New button options, including New Web.

8   Using the same method, create and save two additional empty Web pages. Name the first page Location.htm and name the second page Recreation.htm.

You will use these additional pages later in the lesson.

FP2000.7.1

Adding and Formatting Text

FrontPage makes it easy to add text and other elements to Web pages. To add text, you simply type it on the page. You can then apply standard Web text styles to the text. You can also format text (and other Web page elements) with FrontPage's own formatting tools and styles for headings or body text. The Formatting toolbar even includes some of the same buttons as those in Microsoft Word and other familiar programs.

FrontPage includes more than a dozen ready-made paragraph styles that you can apply to text on Web pages. A **style** is a collection of **formatting attributes** that can be applied to a paragraph by clicking the style name in the Style list (available by clicking the style down arrow on the Formatting tool bar). Attributes include font name, font size, and character appearance.

You can apply formatting attributes separately using buttons, lists, and dialog boxes within FrontPage. But you'll often find that the ready-made styles help you to achieve the text appearance that you want with only a few mouse clicks. For instance, FrontPage includes six styles that apply formatting for different headings and several styles for creating bulleted and numbered lists.

In this exercise, you open the Lakewood Mountains Resort home page for editing. You then add and format text on the page.

1   In the Folder List, double-click the file HomePage.htm.

FrontPage displays the home page in Page view. The page is currently blank.

Other Microsoft Office applications support character styles, which allow you to apply formatting to selected text characters. However, FrontPage supports only paragraph styles, which means that formatting attributes will be applied to all text in selected paragraphs.

2   Type **Lakewood Mountains Resort** (but do not press Enter).

3   Click the Style box down arrow at the left end of the Formatting toolbar.

The Style list shows available paragraph styles.

4   Click Heading 1 in the list, and on the Formatting toolbar, click the Center button.

Center

FrontPage formats the line in the Heading 1 style and centers the heading on the line.

5   Press Enter twice, and type:
1501 Bryant's Gap Trail, Erewhon, CA 94501

tip

Notice the jagged underline under the word *Erewhon*. The underline indicates that the FrontPage spelling checker did not find the word in its dictionary and that it might be misspelled. However, it is the proper name of a town and is spelled correctly. You'll learn how to use FrontPage's spelling checker in Lesson 7, "Publishing a Web"; just ignore the underlining for now.

6   Select the text in the address line.

7   On the Formatting toolbar, click the Bold button.

Bold

FrontPage applies bold formatting to the selected text.

8   On the Standard toolbar, click the Save button.

Save

FrontPage saves your changes. Your page should look similar to the following.

If the heading text will not all fit on one line in a visitor's browser window, the heading will remain centered but will wrap one or more words to the next line.

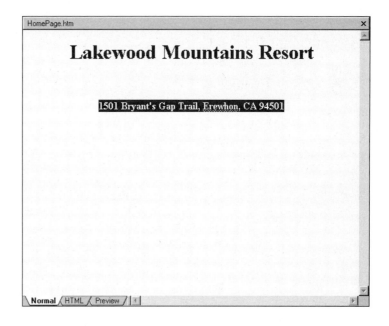

FP2000.5.3

Changing Web Page Properties

The file name for a Web page can be (and usually is) different from the title of the Web page. The title is the text that appears in the title bar of a Web browser and in any **banners** that you create. A banner is a graphic that appears on all or most pages in a Web and is generally used to display the title of the Web itself. FrontPage uses the file name for a page as its title unless you assign it a different title.

In Navigation view, a Web page is displayed as an icon. The name of the icon, by default, is the name of the file. If you want, you can click the icon and change its name so that it is more descriptive. However, changing the name of an icon in Navigation view will not change the file name or the title for the Web page. It's important to recognize, then, that the file name, title, and icon name for a Web page can have different names.

tip

Web servers use different conventions for naming home pages. Most re-quire this file to be named either Default.htm or Index.htm. If your home page name is different from the name that the Web server you're publishing to requires, don't worry; FrontPage automatically renames the home page when you publish a Web to a server. (If you're uploading files manually instead of having FrontPage publish them for you—as you must with popular Web sites such as GeoCities or The Globe—you will have to rename the file yourself.)

In this exercise, you change Web page properties—specifically, you change the title and add a summary comment. As you'll see, you can change a Web page's properties even after it has been created in FrontPage.

1   In the Folder List, right-click the file HomePage.htm, and click Properties on the shortcut menu that appears.

FrontPage displays the Properties dialog box for the file HomePage.htm with the contents of the Title box selected.

Until you save a page with a different name, FrontPage will assign the title *New Page* followed by a number to new pages that you create.

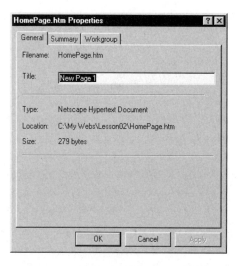

2 In the Title box, type **Lakewood Mountains Resort**, and click the Summary tab.

On the Summary tab in the Comments box, you can write an explanation of the purpose of the current page.

3 Type **This will be the home page for the LMR site**, and click OK.

FrontPage changes the title of the Web page and adds your comment.

Save

4 On the Standard toolbar, click the Save button.

FrontPage saves the home page with its new title.

Previewing a Web Page

When you create Web pages in Page view, FrontPage provides a good representation of what the pages will look like to Web visitors. However, it is a somewhat simplified view. To make sure you know how the pages will look to Web visitors, you should preview them as you work on them. You can preview a Web page in two ways. The quickest way is to click the Preview tab along the bottom of the FrontPage window.

Although this preview takes only a second to appear, it doesn't always show you exactly how a page will look in a particular browser like Microsoft Internet Explorer or Netscape Navigator. A more reliable approach is to use the Preview In Browser button on the Standard toolbar. When you click this button, FrontPage will launch your default Web browser and display the current page within the browser.

In this exercise, you preview the home page that you have created.

1 Click the Preview tab at the bottom of the FrontPage window.

Because the home page currently contains only two lines of text, Preview view does not offer you any additional information.

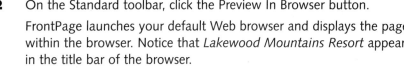

Preview In Browser

2 On the Standard toolbar, click the Preview In Browser button.

FrontPage launches your default Web browser and displays the page within the browser. Notice that *Lakewood Mountains Resort* appears in the title bar of the browser.

Clicking the Preview tab will provide a close approximation of the way a page will appear in viewers' Web browsers. However, the Preview In Browser button provides a way to more precisely see how the pages will look in your default Web browser. To see how the page will appear in other browsers, you need to open the page from within that browser.

Close

3 Click the Close button in the top-right corner of the Web browser.

The browser closes.

FP2000.11.3

Moving and Organizing Files in Folders View

At this point, you have started the creation of a home page, and you have added and named two additional blank pages. Later, you can add text and graphics to these pages. To organize versions and revisions of Web pages in FrontPage, you can add folders and then drag related files into these new folders.

In this exercise, you create a folder for the preliminary pages in the Lakewood Mountains Resort Web.

1   On the Views bar, click the Folders icon.

2   On the File menu, point to New, and click Folder.

A new folder is created in the Contents list of files and folders in the Web.

3   Type **Pages in Work**, and press Enter.

FrontPage creates and names the new folder.

4   Drag the files HomePage, Location, and Recreation to the Pages in Work folder.

5   Double-click the Pages In Work folder to display the three files in Folders view.

Creating temporary pages in the work folder can help you by separating pages that need additional editing from pages that have been completed.

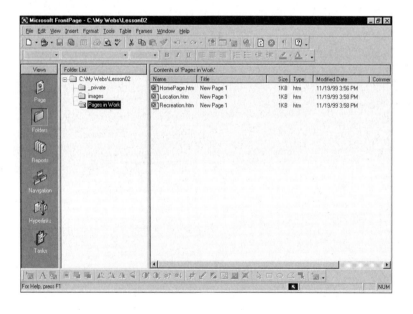

FP2000.11.3

Moving and Organizing Files in Navigation View

Although you now have three pages (HomePage, the Location page, and the Recreation page) in the Web site for Lakewood Mountains Resort, the pages aren't arranged in any particular structure. You know that the home page is the "starting" page, but beyond that, there's no organization to the Web.

In FrontPage, you can structure a Web by dragging Web page files into the Navigation tree diagram. You will see many reasons for using this diagram. First, it makes the Web structure easier to understand. Instead of having to remember which Web pages link to which, you can simply look at the tree diagram.

Another reason has to do with designing the site. You can make FrontPage set up navigation bars to link all the pages displayed in Navigation view. Navigation bars use the information in the tree diagram to link pages. If the tree diagram of the Web isn't accurate, navigation bars won't work correctly.

In this exercise, you create a navigation structure for the Lakewood Mountains Resort Web.

1   On the Views bar, click the Navigation icon.

No icons are displayed in Navigation view.

2   Drag the file HomePage.htm from the Folder List into Navigation view.

The home page icon (which now reads *Lakewood Mountains Resort*) is added to Navigation view.

3   Drag the file Location.htm from the Folder List into Navigation view, below the home page icon.

> If you are in Page view and have a Web page open, dragging a file from the Folder List onto the page will create a link to the dragged page.

A line connects the Lakewood Mountains Resort home page to the Location page. The Location page is a child page (lower-level page) of the home page. Because a title has not been created for this page, the icon displays the default text *New Page 1*.

4   Drag the file Recreation.htm from the Folder List into Navigation view below the Lakewood Mountains Resort home page icon, but to the right of the Location page icon.

A line connects the Lakewood Mountains Resort home page to the Recreation page and the Location page. Because a title has not been created for this page, the icon displays the default text *New Page 1*.

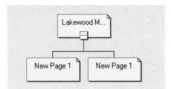

FP2000.11.2

Viewing and Printing a Web Structure

You have seen the advantage of organizing a Web site in Navigation view. Navigation view allows you to drag Web page files into a visual hierarchy. You can take that advantage a step further by using Navigation view to display and print the structure of a Web site.

In this exercise, you display and print the Web site structure.

1   On the File menu, click Print.

The Print dialog box appears.

2   Click OK.

The Web's navigation structure is printed.

tip
You can preview the layout of the navigation structure by clicking Print Preview on the File menu. If the navigation structure of the Web is too large to fit on a single page, close the Print Preview window and right-click any blank area in Navigation view. Click Rotate on the shortcut menu to switch the page orientation of the tree diagram.

Lesson Wrap-Up

This lesson covered how to create a Web site, create a new Web page, add and format Web page text, add pages to a Web, change Web properties, preview a Web page, organize a Web, and view and print a Web structure.

If you are continuing to the next lesson:

●   On the File menu, click Close Web. If FrontPage prompts you to save changes, click Yes.

FrontPage saves any changes and closes the LakewoodDemo Web.

If you are not continuing to other lessons:

Close

● Click the Close button in the top-right corner of the FrontPage window. If FrontPage prompts you to save changes, click Yes. FrontPage saves any changes, closes the Web, and then exits.

Lesson Glossary

banner A graphic that appears on all or most pages in a Web and is generally used to display the title of the Web itself.

empty Web A folder structure that FrontPage creates for a Web, with no pages created.

feedback form A Web page that allows site visitors to type comments about a Web site and send them to an e-mail address that you specify.

formatting attributes Characteristics of text, such as bold font, italics, font size, or text color.

one-page Web A Web site with only a home page.

personal Web A Web site to showcase the interests of an individual. It includes a home page, a photo album page, an interests page, and a Web page for links to other Web sites.

preview A way to view a Web page to see how it will look to Web visitors.

project Web A Web site that shares information about a project with members of a project team. It includes a page that lists team members, a schedule page, a project status page, a message board, and a search page.

search form A list that allows Web site visitors to search the Web site for pages containing words that they specify.

style A collection of formatting attributes that can be applied to selected paragraphs by clicking the Style down arrow on the Formatting toolbar and then clicking the desired style name.

templates Ready-made Web pages containing all the formatting required to build a page.

wizard A collection of dialog boxes in which FrontPage requests that you enter information to be used in creating a Web site or Web page.

Quick Quiz

1   As you add Web pages, which FrontPage views are best for organizing and maintaining your Web site?

2   A _____ creates the layout for a particular kind of Web or page and includes placeholder text.

3   A _____ creates a Web using a series of dialog boxes in which you select the specific options that fit your situation.

4   What are three basic ways to create a Web in FrontPage?

5   If you have a previous version of your Web, is it better to: (a) create a new Web based on your existing files, or: (b) create other files after you create the Web itself?

Putting It All Together

Exercise 1: You have been asked to build a set of Discussion Web pages for the Lakewood Mountains Resort Web site. Use the Discussion Web Wizard to create these pages. Include a Table of Contents page and a Threaded Replies page. Title the discussion *LMR Web Discussion*. For input fields, use Subject and Comments. Allow anybody to post messages to the discussion. Sort the table of contents by oldest to newest messages, and make the table of contents the home page. Do not include a Web theme.

Exercise 2: The Location Web page for the Lakewood Mountains Resort Web site needs some additional opening text. Reopen the LakewoodDemo Web, and add the following lines of text to the home page:

Welcome to your home away from home. Please tour our site to find out more about what we have to offer.

Left-align the text. Italicize the text and make it green.

LESSON 3

Linking Web Pages

After completing this lesson, you will be able to:

✔ *Create hyperlinks between Web pages.*

✔ *Link to Web pages on the Internet.*

✔ *Test hyperlinks.*

✔ *Create e-mail hyperlinks.*

✔ *Edit hyperlinks.*

✔ *Create Web page bookmarks.*

✔ *Create image map hyperlinks.*

A **hyperlink**, often called a *link*, is a crucial part of any Web site. Hyperlinks are the connections between elements on Web pages; they're what make "surfing" the Internet possible. On a Web page, a hyperlink can be a word, a phrase, a symbol, or an image. Hyperlinks make it easy for visitors to get the information that they need by providing seamless navigation from one Web page to another.

In this lesson, you will learn how to create several kinds of hyperlinks: hyperlinks between Web pages, hyperlinks to pages on the Internet, and e-mail hyperlinks. You will also learn how to create and use bookmarks on a Web page. Finally, you will create a special kind of hyperlink called an image map.

Sample files for the lesson

To complete the procedures in this lesson, you will need to create a new Web based on the files in the Lesson03 folder in the FrontPage Core Practice folder that is located on your hard disk. You will use this Web for all the exercises in Lesson 3.

If your hard disk uses a letter other than C, substitute the appropriate drive letter in place of C.

For the complete steps on importing a Web, see the "Using the CD-ROM" section at the beginning of this book or refer to the Lesson 1 section "Creating and Importing Webs."

1 On the File menu, point to New, and click Web.

2 Click the Import Wizard icon.

3 In the Specify The Location Of The New Web box, delete the default text, and type **C:\My Webs\Lesson03**.

4 Click OK to continue.

FP2000.7.4

Pointing Hand

Linking to a Web Page in the Current Web

A hyperlink is an HTML instruction embedded in a Web page. The instruction tells a Web browser to display another file or Web page when the visitor clicks the corresponding text or graphic. The newly displayed file can be a Web page stored on a Web server, a Web page on a corporate intranet, or a file stored locally on the visitor's computer.

Each hyperlink has two parts: the hyperlink itself and the **target**, which is the file displayed after a visitor clicks the hyperlink. When a user moves the mouse pointer over a hyperlink, the pointer changes from its normal shape to a pointing hand. This tells the visitor that the pointer is over a hyperlink. The status bar at the bottom of the user's Web browser usually displays the address of the target when the mouse is over a hyperlink.

With FrontPage, the process of creating hyperlinks is straightforward and quick. To create hyperlinks, you just point and click. FrontPage takes care of the details.

In this exercise, you create a hyperlink between the Lakewood Mountains Resort home page and its Recreation page.

1   In the Folder List, double-click the file Index.htm.

FrontPage displays the home page in Page view.

2   On the home page, select the word *Recreation*.

3   On the Insert menu, click Hyperlink.

FrontPage displays the Create Hyperlink dialog box.

Ctrl+K is the keyboard shortcut to create a hyperlink for selected text or a selected graphic. First, select the text or graphic, and then press Ctrl+K to display the Create Hyperlink dialog box.

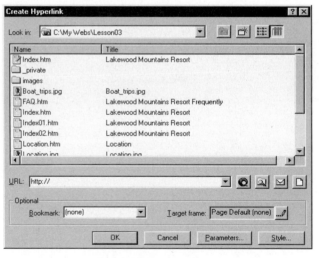

4   In the File list, scroll down and click Recreati.htm.

FrontPage displays Recreati.htm in the URL box. This is the target of the hyperlink.

5 Click OK. Deselect the word *Recreation* by clicking any blank area of the home page.

FrontPage creates the hyperlink. Notice that the word *Recreation* is now underlined, indicating that it is a hyperlink.

To test a hyperlink, hold down Ctrl and click the hyperlink.

Hyperlink

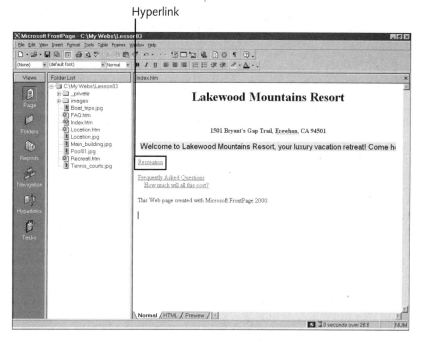

Save

6 On the Standard toolbar, click the Save button.

FrontPage saves the changes.

> ## tip
>
> When you position the mouse pointer over a hyperlink, FrontPage displays the link target address on the status bar in the bottom-right corner of the screen. You can check that a hyperlink is functioning by pressing Ctrl and clicking the hyperlink image or text. FrontPage will then display the target page in the viewing area. In a later exercise, you will preview links in a Web browser.

FP2000.7.4

Linking to a Web Page on the Internet

When you create links to sites outside your Web, you add versatility to the Web. Visitors realize that you have their interests in mind because you make it easy for them to obtain additional information.

For example, visitors to the Lakewood Mountains Resort Web site might like to find out about the town of Erewhon, where the resort is located. You don't have the time or resources to create a series of Web pages describing the town. Instead, you could browse the Internet to find the Erewhon city Web site and create a link to it.

In this exercise, you create a hyperlink to the Microsoft FrontPage home page on the Internet.

1   Select the word *Microsoft* in the last line on the home page.

2   On the Insert menu, click Hyperlink.

FrontPage displays the Create Hyperlink dialog box.

Web Browser

3   Click the Use Your Web Browser To Select A Page Or File button.

FrontPage opens your default Web browser and instructs you to browse to the Web page to which you want to link.

4   In the Address bar of the Web browser, type **www.microsoft.com/ frontpage**, and press Enter.

The Web browser displays the FrontPage home page.

5   Press Alt+Tab on the keyboard to switch from the browser to FrontPage.

In the URL box, FrontPage displays the Web address of the Microsoft FrontPage home page, as shown in the illustration.

Web addresses change frequently. The URL box might display a different redirected Web page address. A redirected address is one in which the Web server links the address you have typed to the new address for the page.

Save

6   Click OK. On the Standard toolbar, click the Save button.

FrontPage creates the hyperlink and saves your changes.

FP2000.12.3

Testing Hyperlinks

Making certain that hyperlinks work is very important. There is nothing more frustrating to a visitor than clicking a link only to find the wrong file, or perhaps no file at all, displayed in the browser.

In this exercise, you test the hyperlink to the FrontPage home page that you created to make certain that it is accurate.

Preview In Browser

1   On the Standard toolbar, click the Preview In Browser button, and click the button for your Web browser on the taskbar.

Your Web browser displays the home page.

2 Click the *Recreation* hyperlink.

The Web browser displays the Recreation page.

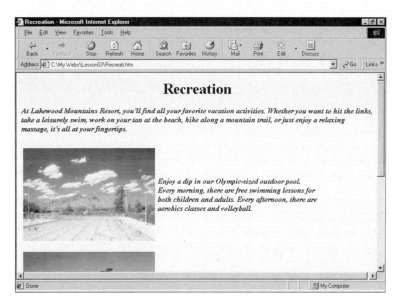

Back

3 On the toolbar of the Web browser, click the Back button.

The Web browser displays the Lakewood Mountains Resort home page.

4 Click the *Microsoft* hyperlink.

The Web browser displays the Microsoft FrontPage home page.

Close

5 Click the Close button in the top-right corner of the Web browser window.

The Web browser closes, and FrontPage reappears.

Creating a Hyperlink to an E-Mail Address

Hyperlinks do more than simply display a Web page or file. Hyperlinks also provide a way for Web site visitors to send e-mail to the address specified in the hyperlink. When a visitor clicks an **e-mail hyperlink,** the Web browser starts the visitor's e-mail program and displays a message composition window with the e-mail address already entered. The visitor then writes and sends the e-mail message as he or she would any e-mail message.

You want visitors to the Lakewood Mountains Resort Web site to be able to send e-mail messages to the resort's Webmaster, so you need to create a link to the Webmaster's e-mail address.

In this exercise, you create a hyperlink that enables a Web page visitor to send e-mail messages to the Lakewood Mountain Resort Webmaster.

1 Click the empty line below the *Microsoft* hyperlink.

2 Type **Send e-mail to Lakewood Webmaster**, and select the words *Lakewood Webmaster*.

3   On the Insert menu, click Hyperlink.

FrontPage displays the Create Hyperlink dialog box.

E-mail

4   In the Create Hyperlink dialog box, click the Make A Hyperlink That Sends E-mail button.

FrontPage displays the Create E-mail Hyperlink dialog box.

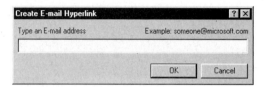

If you do not have an e-mail address, use *someone@microsoft.com*.

5   In the Type An E-mail Address box, type your own e-mail address, and click OK.

The Create E-mail Hyperlink dialog box closes, and the Create Hyperlink dialog box is again visible. Notice that the URL contains the text *mailto:* followed by the e-mail address you just typed.

6   Click OK, and click the Save button on the Standard toolbar.

FrontPage creates the new e-mail hyperlink and saves your changes.

Editing a Hyperlink

Hyperlink targets often change. For example, the name of a Web page file might change, or a Web page might be moved to a different Web site. When such a change occurs, you need to change any hyperlinks that connect to the target file. Fortunately changing a hyperlink in FrontPage is just as easy as creating it in the first place.

In this exercise, you change the target Web page of the Frequently Asked Questions hyperlink. You then change the text of the Location hyperlink and delete the Lakewood Webmaster hyperlink.

1   Right-click the Frequently Asked Questions hyperlink, and click Hyperlink Properties on the shortcut menu.

FrontPage displays the Edit Hyperlink dialog box. Notice that the Frequently Asked Questions link has the Location page as its target in the URL box. The Location page is an incorrect target for this link.

The Bookmark box allows you to create a hyperlink to a previously created bookmark on the current page. To create a bookmark, position the insertion point at the location you want to bookmark, click Bookmark on the Insert menu, and type a name for the bookmark. Bookmarks are explained in the next section of this lesson.

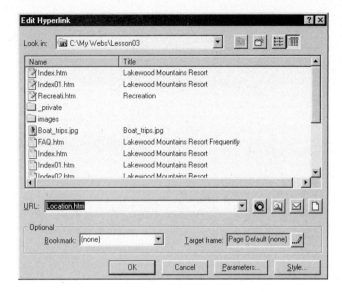

2 Click FAQ.htm in the file list, and click OK.

FrontPage changes the target page to the FAQ page.

3 Click any blank area of the page to deselect the link. Check the Frequently Asked Questions link by pressing Ctrl and clicking the link.

FrontPage displays the FAQ page.

Close

4 Click the Close button in the top-right corner of the FAQ page.

FrontPage closes the FAQ page and displays the home page.

5 Double-click the *Recreation* hyperlink, and type **Resort Activities**.

The new text replaces the old text, leaving the hyperlink intact.

6 Right-click the *Lakewood Webmaster* hyperlink.

FrontPage displays a shortcut menu.

7 On the shortcut menu, click Hyperlink Properties.

FrontPage displays the Edit Hyperlink dialog box. The URL text is selected.

8 Press Delete, and click OK.

FrontPage deletes the URL text from the text box and removes the hyperlink from the Web page text. Notice that the text is no longer underlined.

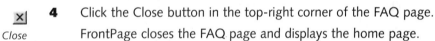

Save

9 On the Standard toolbar, click the Save button.

FrontPage saves your changes.

tip

You can also delete a hyperlink by selecting the hyperlink text on the Web page, and pressing delete. Both the text and the hyperlink will be removed from the Web page.

Creating a Bookmark on a Web Page

Normally, when visitors click a hyperlink to a Web page, their browsers display only as much of the page as fits in the browser window. If the Web page is longer than a single screen, visitors must scroll down the page to see all of the content. For lengthy Web pages, this process is cumbersome.

A **bookmark** can help solve this problem. In FrontPage, a bookmark is a link to a specific location on a Web page. Because the Lakewood Mountains Resort FAQ page is very long, bookmarks make it easier for Web site visitors to navigate through the page.

In this exercise, you create bookmarks on the FAQ Web page. You then link from one location on the FAQ Web page to a bookmark at another location on the same Web page.

1   In the Folder List, double-click the file FAQ.htm.

FrontPage displays the FAQ page in Page view.

> If you double-click the name of a picture (which has the extension .gif or .jpg) in the Folder List, FrontPage will display the picture in the program that has picture file name extensions assigned to it.

2   Scroll down to the end of the FAQ page.

FrontPage displays the question *How much will all this cost?* and its answer.

3   Select the text *How much will all this cost?*

> Prior to creating a bookmark, you must either select the bookmark text or position the insertion point where you want the bookmark to link to.

Bookmark

tip

You do not have to select text for a bookmark. You can simply place the insertion point where you want the bookmark, click Bookmark on the Insert menu, type a name for the bookmark, and then click OK. When a location is marked for a bookmark, FrontPage identifies the bookmark position with the Bookmark symbol.

4 On the Insert menu, click Bookmark.

FrontPage displays the Bookmark dialog box.

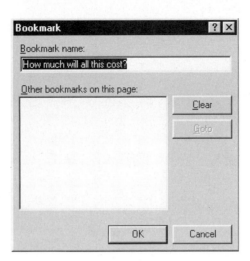

5 Click OK, and deselect the text by clicking any blank area of the FAQ page.

FrontPage creates the bookmark. Notice that the text is now underlined with a broken line. The broken underline distinguishes it from the solid underline displayed by a hyperlink.

6 Scroll up to the paragraph with the heading *How's the food?*, and select the text *How's the food?*

7 On the Insert menu, click Bookmark, and click OK.

8 Deselect the text by clicking any blank area of the FAQ page.

9 Scroll up to the numbered list of questions at the top of the FAQ page.

10 In the list, select the text *How's the food?*

11 On the Insert menu, click Hyperlink, and click FAQ.htm in the dialog box's file list.

You will test these bookmarks later in this lesson.

12 Click the Bookmark down arrow, click *How's the food?*, and then click OK.

FrontPage inserts the bookmark.

Save

13 On the Standard toolbar, click the Save button.

FrontPage saves your changes.

Creating a Hyperlink to a Bookmark

In the previous exercise, you learned how bookmarks make it easy for visitors to navigate a Web page. But impatient visitors to the Lakewood Mountains Resort site might not want to spend time searching the site for an FAQ page to find out how much they'll need to pay for a stay at the resort. You can solve this problem easily by using a hyperlink.

Hyperlinks do more than link the top of one Web page to the top of another Web page. Creating a hyperlink from a Web page to a specific point on another Web page—using a bookmark—makes it easy for visitors to quickly find information on a Web site.

In this exercise, you create a hyperlink from the Lakewood Mountains Resort home page to the *How much will all this cost?* bookmark on the FAQ page.

You can only create a bookmark to a different location on the current page. You can't create a bookmark to a different page in the Web.

1 In the Folder List, double-click the file Index.htm.

FrontPage displays the home page in Page view.

2 Select the text *How much will it cost?*

3 On the Insert menu, click Hyperlink.

FrontPage displays the Create Hyperlink dialog box.

4 In the file list, click FAQ.htm.

5 Click the Bookmark down arrow at the bottom of the dialog box.

FrontPage displays a list of bookmarks on the FAQ page.

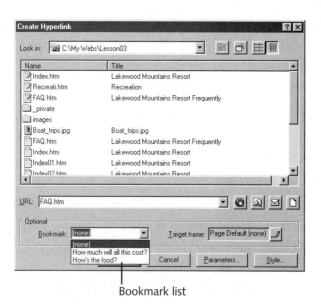

Bookmark list

You will test this hyperlink in the next exercise in this lesson.

Save

6 Click How much will all this cost?, and click OK.

FrontPage inserts the hyperlink.

7 On the Standard toolbar, click the Save button.

FrontPage saves your changes.

Testing a Bookmark

It is just as important to test bookmarks as it is to test hyperlinks. Remember that when you create a bookmark, you aren't required to target text on the Web page. For this reason, you should check all the bookmarks you create to ensure that visitors don't get frustrated by using bookmarks that take them to the wrong place on a page.

In this exercise, you test the bookmarks that you created to make certain they work.

Preview In Browser

1 On the Standard toolbar, click the Preview In Browser button.

FrontPage displays the home page in your default Web browser. The

FrontPage creates a bookmark by inserting an <a name> HTML tag in the file. You can view this tag by clicking the HTML tab.

home page should look similar to the following illustration.

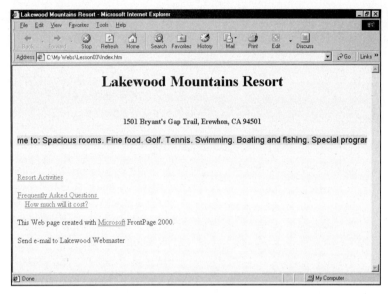

2 Click the *How much will it cost?* hyperlink.

The Web browser displays the final question on the FAQ Web page.

3 Scroll to the top of the FAQ page.

4 Click the *How's the food?* hyperlink.

The Web browser displays the *How's the food?* bookmark.

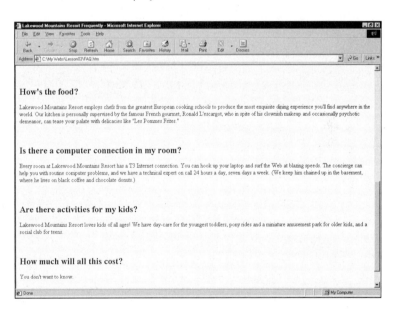

✕

Close

5 Click the Close button in the top-right corner of the Web browser window.

The Web browser closes, and FrontPage reappears.

Deleting a Bookmark

While updating a Web site, you might decide that certain bookmarks are no longer needed. For example, suppose you find that you have deleted so much content from a page that all the remaining material fits on one screen. You would no longer need to use bookmarks on that page to save visitors from having to scroll down the page. Using FrontPage, it is just as easy to delete a bookmark as it is to create one.

In this exercise, you delete the *How's the food?* bookmark from the Lakewood Mountains Resort FAQ page.

1 In the Folder List, double-click the file FAQ.htm.

FrontPage displays the FAQ page in Page view.

2 If necessary, scroll down to display the *How's the food?* bookmark (not the hyperlink).

3 Right-click the bookmark text, and click Bookmark Properties on the shortcut menu.

FrontPage displays the Bookmark dialog box.

> If you forget the location of a bookmark that you've created, click Bookmark on the Insert menu, click the name of the bookmark in the list, and then click Go To. FrontPage will display the location of the bookmark.

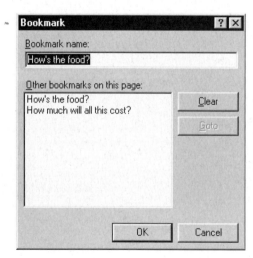

4 In the Other Bookmarks On This Page list, click *How's the food?*, and click Clear.

FrontPage deletes the bookmark.

Save

5 On the Standard toolbar, click the Save button.

FrontPage saves your changes.

FP2000.8.3

Creating and Testing an Image Map

An **image map** allows visitors to a Web site to click a portion of an image—called a **hot spot**—to display the Web page connected with that part of the image. This is a feature that dramatically increases the versatility of most Web sites because it provides visitors with an exciting, visual way to find and display Web pages.

FrontPage makes it easy to create image maps. All you have to do is insert an image on a Web page, draw hotspots, create a few hyperlinks, and your image map is created.

In this exercise, you insert an image of the hotel building on the Lakewood Mountains Resort home page, create an image map, and then test the image map.

1 In the Folder List, double-click the file Index.htm.

FrontPage displays the Lakewood Mountains Resort home page.

2 Click the line below the text *Lakewood Mountains Resort* and above the address of the resort.

3 On the Insert menu, point to Picture, and click From File.

FrontPage displays the Picture dialog box.

4 In the file list, click Main_building.jpg.

FrontPage displays a preview of the image in the preview pane.

> Usually the title of a picture is the same as the file name for the picture. However, you can change the title for a picture by right-clicking the name of the picture in the Folder List, clicking Properties, and then typing a new title in the Title box.

Picture

Look in: C:\My Webs\Lesson03

Name	Title
_private	
images	
Boat_trips.jpg	Boat_trips.jpg
Location.jpg	Location.jpg
Main_building.jpg	Main_building.jpg
Pool01.jpg	Pool01.jpg
Tennis_courts.jpg	Tennis_courts.jpg

URL: Main_building.jpg

OK   Cancel   Clip Art...   Parameters...   Scan...

5 Click OK.

FrontPage inserts the image at the location that you selected.

6 Click the Resort image to select it.

FrontPage displays the Pictures toolbar along the bottom of the screen.

Rectangular Hotspot

7 On the Pictures toolbar, click the Rectangular Hotspot button.

8 Hold down the left mouse button, and drag the mouse pointer to draw a rectangle on the grassy area in front of the hotel building.

FrontPage displays the Create Hyperlink dialog box.

Rectangular Hotspot

9 In the file list, click the file Recreati.htm, and click OK.

FrontPage inserts a hyperlink on the image area that you selected.

10   Click the Rectangular Hotspot button, and draw another rectangle, this time on the hotel building.

FrontPage displays the Create Hyperlink dialog box.

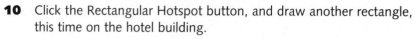
Save

11   In the file list, click the file Location.htm, and click OK.

FrontPage inserts another hyperlink on the image.

Preview in Browser

12   On the Standard toolbar, click the Save button.

FrontPage saves your changes.

13   On the Standard toolbar, click the Preview In Browser button.

FrontPage displays the home page in your Web browser.

> The Pictures toolbar appears only when you click an image. When you click outside the image, the Pictures toolbar no longer appears. If you want to keep the Pictures toolbar displayed, click anywhere outside an image, point to Toolbars on the View menu, and then click Pictures.

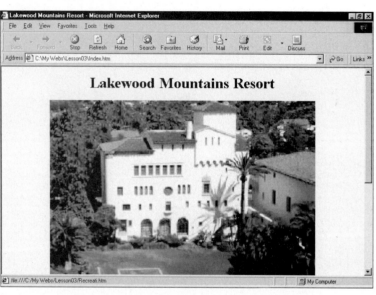

Pointing Hand

14   Move the mouse pointer over the image, but do not click the mouse button.

Over the hotspots, the mouse pointer turns from an arrow to a pointing hand, indicating the presence of hyperlinks.

Back

15   Click the grassy area hotspot.

The Web browser displays the Recreation page.

Close

16   On the toolbar of the Web browser, click the Back button, and click the hotel building hotspot.

The Web browser displays the Location page.

17   Click the Close button in the top-right corner of the Web browser window.

The browser closes, and FrontPage appears.

Lesson Wrap-Up

This lesson covered a variety of uses for hyperlinks. You learned how to create, change, and delete a text hyperlink. You learned how to create and use an e-mail hyperlink. You also learned how to create and delete bookmarks, and how to create an image map on a Web page.

If you are continuing to the next lesson:

X

Close

- On the File menu, click Close Web. If FrontPage prompts you to save changes, click Yes.

  FrontPage saves your changes and closes the Lesson03 Web.

If you are not continuing to other lessons:

- Click the Close button in the top-right corner of the FrontPage window. If FrontPage prompts you to save changes, click Yes.

  FrontPage saves your changes, closes the Web, and then exits.

Lesson Glossary

bookmark A location or selected text on a Web page marked as a target for a hyperlink.

e-mail hyperlink An HTML instruction embedded in a Web page that tells a Web browser to launch the visitor's e-mail program when the hyperlink is clicked.

hot spot An area of an image with an embedded hyperlink.

hyperlinks HTML instructions embedded in a Web page that tell a Web browser to display another Web page when the text is clicked.

image map A graphic image containing hot spots used to link to different Web pages.

target The file that is displayed after a visitor clicks a hyperlink.

Quick Quiz

1   What feature do you use to make it easy to move between pages in a Web?

2   When would you use an e-mail hyperlink?

3   Are you required to select text to create a bookmark?

4   Why is it necessary to test a hyperlink?

5   How do you check a hyperlink in FrontPage?

Putting It All Together

Exercise 1: Create a bookmark for the text *Where is Lakewood Mountains Resort?* on the FAQ page in the Lesson03 Web. On the home page, create a hotspot on the hotel building image that links to the bookmark you just created.

Exercise 2: Create a new page called Comments and Suggestions. Edit the *Send e-mail to Lakewood Webmaster* text and hyperlink so that a visitor's browser displays the Comments and Suggestions page when the link is clicked.

LESSON 4

Adding Style to Web Pages

After completing this lesson, you will be able to:

✔ Apply a FrontPage theme to a Web.

✔ Modify a theme.

✔ Delete a theme from an entire Web.

✔ Add a marquee to a Web page.

✔ Customize a marquee.

✔ Format marquee text.

✔ Add a hit counter to a Web page.

✔ Include one Web page inside another.

✔ Create a style.

✔ Use the Format Painter.

Text and hyperlinks are the backbone of a Web, but when you design a Web, you want to be sure that it attracts visitors. Using Microsoft FrontPage, you can easily create a "look" for a Web that uses pleasing and stylish graphical elements to emphasize content.

In this lesson, you will discover how easy it is to style a Web site using FrontPage. You will learn how to apply FrontPage themes to give a consistent look to all of the pages in a Web. You will also learn how to use FrontPage components to display hit counters, Web page banners, and other elements that help a Web page stand out. Finally, you will learn how to use Web page style sheets to format Web pages.

Sample files for the lesson

To complete the procedures in this lesson, you will need to create a new Web based on the files in the Lesson04 folder in the FrontPage Core Practice folder that is located on your hard disk. You will use this Web for all the exercises in Lesson 4.

If your hard disk uses a letter other than C, substitute the appropriate drive letter in place of C.

For the complete steps on importing a Web, see the "Using the CD-ROM" section at the beginning of this book or refer to the Lesson 1 section "Creating and Importing Webs."

1   On the File menu, point to New, and click Web.

2   Click the Import Web Wizard icon.

3   In the Specify The Location Of The New Web box, delete the default text, and type **C:\My Webs\Lesson04**.

4   Click OK to continue.

FP2000.3.1

Applying a FrontPage Theme to a Web

A **theme** is a unified set of design elements and color schemes that you apply to Web pages to give the pages a consistent and attractive appearance. When you apply a theme to a Web, all the pages in the Web (and any new pages that you create) share a common color scheme and background. The pages also share the same design for navigation bars, buttons, and other Web page elements.

In this exercise, you apply the Expedition theme to all the pages of the Lakewood Mountains Resort Web.

1   In the Folder List, double-click the file Welcome.htm.

FrontPage displays the home page.

2   On the Format menu, click Theme.

FrontPage displays the Themes dialog box with No Theme selected.

Notice the Apply Theme To options near the top-left corner of the dialog box. All Pages is selected by default, but you can use the Selected Page(s) option to apply a theme to only the current page or a group of pages.

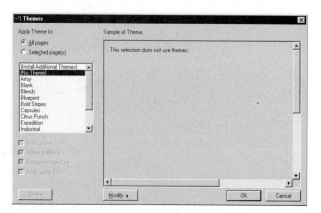

3   In the Themes list, click Artsy.

FrontPage displays a sample of how Web page elements look with the Artsy theme.

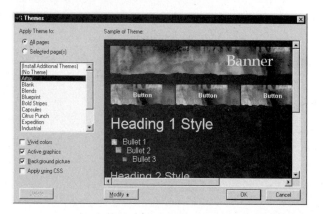

4 In the Themes list, click Rice Paper.

FrontPage displays a sample of how Web page elements look with the Rice Paper theme.

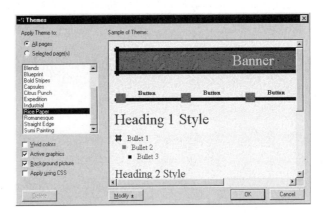

5 In the Themes list, click Expedition.

FrontPage displays a sample of how Web page elements look with the Expedition theme.

The Modify button (which you will use later) allows you to change the colors for theme components, change the graphics used for theme components, and change the text font for the theme.

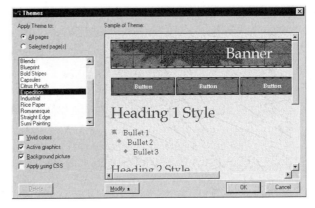

6 Select the Vivid Colors check box.

FrontPage changes the appearance of Web page elements in the sample.

7 Clear the Background Picture check box.

FrontPage displays a sample of how Web pages look without the background picture.

8 Select the Background Picture check box.

FrontPage restores the background picture.

9 Click OK. If FrontPage displays an alert box asking if you want to apply the theme, click Yes.

FrontPage applies the Expedition theme to all the Web pages in the Lesson04 Web.

Save

10 On the Standard toolbar, click the Save button.

FrontPage saves your changes to the Web.

tip
You can apply a background image to a Web page without using a theme. To do so, display the Web page in Page view, and click Background on the Format menu. In the Page Properties dialog box, click the Background tab, select the Background Picture check box, and then click the Browse button. Browse to the image you want, and click OK twice. Note that the image you select will appear as a repeating tile in the background of the Web page.

Modifying a Theme

After applying a theme, it's often a good idea to modify the theme to give the Web a unique design that is specific to the Web's purpose. You might find that some design elements work better than others for showcasing the Web's content, or that some of the theme's graphics clash with images that you've added to the Web.

In this exercise, you temporarily modify the Expedition theme by changing the Heading 1 font.

You can customize the colors, logos, graphics, backgrounds, and bullets of any ready-made theme to make your own design.

1   On the Format menu, click Theme.

FrontPage displays the Themes dialog box with a sample of the Web's current theme.

2   Click Modify.

The Themes dialog box displays a row of buttons labeled What Would You Like To Modify?

The Color Schemes tab allows you to select a different set of scheme colors, and the Color Wheel tab allows you to select a custom color scheme by dragging the selector on a color wheel.

3   Click the Colors button, click the Custom tab in the Modify Theme dialog box, and then click the Item down arrow.

FrontPage displays a list of Web page items whose color you can change.

4   Click any blank area of the Modify Theme dialog box to close the list, and click Cancel.

The Modify Theme dialog box closes.

5   Click the Graphics button, and click the Item down arrow.

FrontPage displays a list of graphic elements whose appearance you can change.

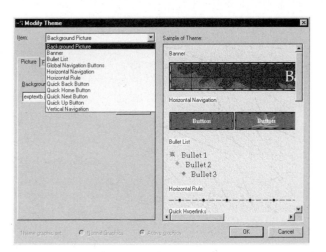

6   Click any blank area of the Modify Theme dialog box, and click Cancel.

The Modify Theme dialog box closes.

7   Click the Text button.

FrontPage displays the Modify Theme dialog box.

8   Click the Item down arrow, and click Heading 1.

9   In the Font list, click Comic Sans MS.

FrontPage changes the font of the Heading 1 style to Comic Sans MS.

You can click the More Text Styles button to display a list of additional paragraph styles. When you click the More Text Styles button to display the Styles dialog box, a Modify button will appear, which you can click to change style attributes, including text color.

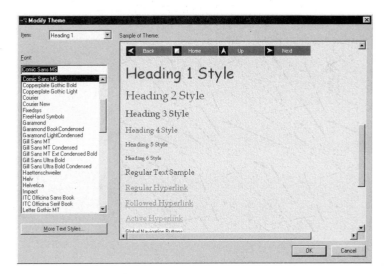

10   Click OK, and click Cancel so that you do not permanently modify the theme.

FrontPage closes the dialog box without saving your changes.

Deleting a Theme from an Entire Web

As you update and modify a Web, you might decide that it's also necessary to make some design changes. You might want to keep the pages that you developed but remove a theme that is no longer appropriate. FrontPage makes it easy to remove a theme from a Web without changing the content of the Web pages.

In this exercise, you delete the Expedition theme from the entire Lakewood Mountains Resort Web without changing the content of the pages that make up the Web.

Close

1   Click the Close button in the top-right corner of the Welcome page.

FrontPage closes the Welcome page.

2   On the Views bar, click the Navigation icon.

FrontPage displays the Web in Navigation view.

3   On the Format menu, click Theme.

FrontPage displays the Themes dialog box. The Expedition theme is selected.

> You can also remove a theme from all Web pages in Page view. Navigation view is shown here to demonstrate another approach.

4   In the Apply Theme To section of the dialog box, verify that the All Pages option is selected.

FrontPage will apply any changes to all pages in the Web.

5   In the Themes list, click No Theme, and click OK.

FrontPage removes the theme from the entire Web.

tip

To remove a theme from an individual Web page, display the Web page in Page view, and click Theme on the Format menu. In the Themes dialog box, click the Selected Pages option, click No Theme in the Themes list, and then click OK.

Adding FrontPage Components

FrontPage **components** are ready-to-use programs that are activated when a visitor loads a page into his or her browser. Components provide a quick and easy way to build features into Web pages without having to learn Web page scripting or ActiveX and Java programming. Some components included with FrontPage are summarized in the following table.

(continued)

continued

If you are unsure whether your Web host supports the FrontPage Server Extensions, avoid using any components that have an asterisk next to their name in the table.

Adding FrontPage Components

Component	Description
Comment	Inserts a comment into a Web page's HTML code to explain some aspect of the coding or design. The comment is invisible when the page is viewed in a browser, though it is visible in FrontPage. The Comment component is useful for annotating a page as you work on it.
Page Banner*	Inserts a graphical banner at the top of a Web page.
Banner Ad Manager	Rotates the display of multiple images at specified intervals. Allows you to select the type of transition between banner ads (dissolve, horizontal blinds, and so on) on a Web page.
Hit Counter*	Displays the number of times that a page has been visited, or "hit."
Hover Button	Inserts a link that displays a visual effect when the mouse pointer "hovers," or is positioned over it. Effects include changing color and appearing to be pressed like a button.
Marquee	Displays text that scrolls horizontally on the Web page.
Confirmation	Confirms a user's entry on a Web page form.
Include Page	Inserts a Web page at a specified location inside another page. For example, you might insert a copyright page at the bottom of every other page in your Web.
Scheduled Include Page*	Inserts a Web page inside another page for a specified period of time and optionally replaces it at a specified time. Useful for displaying time-critical information, such as notification of a seasonal sale.
Substitution	Replaces a section of text with a specified value, such as another text string.
Categories	Inserts links to pages by category. Useful for creating tables of contents for pages of a certain type, such as expense reports or planning.
Search Form*	Allows visitors to search the site for specified text. When you save a page with a search form, FrontPage builds an index of the site. When visitors perform a search, FrontPage uses the index to create a list of hyperlinks to pages containing the word or phrase.
Table of Contents	Creates a table of contents for a Web.

*Components requiring a Web server that supports the FrontPage Server Extensions.

FP2000.10.3

Adding a Marquee to a Web Page

You can easily add impressive features to Web pages to make them stand out. For example, a scrolling **marquee** displays text that slowly moves across the screen. This provides an eye-catching way to showcase a marketing message for Web site visitors. However, use marquees and other animations sparingly; numerous studies of Web visitors report that many people find Web sites that have excessive motion, animation, and blinking to be annoying.

The Impact Public Relations marketing team has created some catchy text that the Lakewood Mountains Resort uses to give unity to all its advertisements. You decide to use a scrolling marquee on the Web's home page to display the text so that visitors will immediately see the marketing message.

In this exercise, you add a marquee to the Lakewood Mountains Resort home page.

1   In the Folder List, double-click the file Welcome.htm.

2   Click at the end of the address line, and press Enter.

FrontPage moves the insertion point to the next line.

3   On the Insert menu, point to Component, and click Marquee.

FrontPage displays the Marquee Properties dialog box.

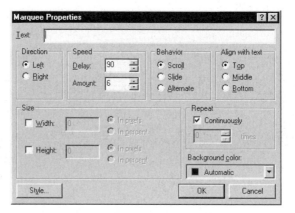

Some components will be displayed differently in Netscape Navigator. For instance, a marquee will be formatted correctly in Netscape Navigator, but the text will not scroll. Always test your Web pages in both Internet Explorer and Netscape Navigator.

4   In the Text box, type the following:

Welcome to Lakewood Mountains Resort, your luxury vacation retreat! Come home to: Spacious rooms. Fine food. Golf. Tennis. Swimming. Boating and fishing. Special programs for kids. And surprisingly low rates!

5   Click OK.

FrontPage places the marquee on the Web page. Only part of the text is visible, and it isn't scrolling. The text will scroll to the left when the page is displayed in a Web browser. You'll preview the marquee later in this lesson.

Customizing a Marquee

A custom marquee brings a bit of distinction and flair to a Web page. You can adjust the speed and direction of the marquee's text movement. You can also change the marquee's width and its background color to make it stand out—or to make it less intrusive.

In this exercise, you change the width and background color of the marquee.

1   Right-click the marquee, and click Marquee Properties on the shortcut menu.

FrontPage displays the Marquee Properties dialog box.

The In Percent option allows you to specify the width of the marquee as a percentage of a visitor's browser window. This option can help your marquee to be displayed properly regardless of the width of visitors' browser windows or screens. Also note the additional Behavior options. The Slide option causes the marquee text to scroll until the opposite end of the marquee region is reached, at which point the text remains on the screen and scrolling stops. The Alternate option allows the marquee to alternate between scrolling and sliding.

2   In the Size section of the dialog box, select the Width check box, select the text in the Width box, type **400**, and then verify that the In Pixels option is selected.

The marquee width is set to 400 pixels.

3   Click the Background Color down arrow.

The Background Color palette expands.

4   Click the Yellow square, and click OK.

FrontPage closes the Marquee Properties dialog box and changes the background color of the marquee to yellow.

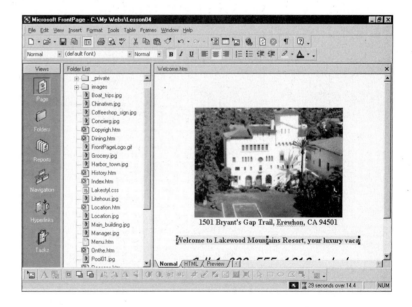

Formatting Marquee Text

Another way to emphasize a marquee is by formatting the text displayed in the marquee. You can make the text stand out and capture the attention of visitors by selecting a custom font or using a different font color.

In this exercise, you change the font and size of the marquee text.

1   Right-click the marquee, and click Font on the shortcut menu.

FrontPage displays the Font dialog box.

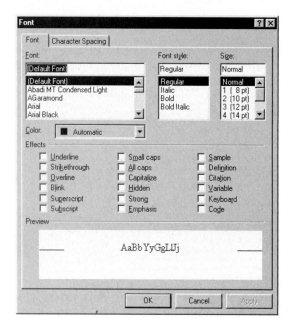

2   In the Font list, click Arial.

FrontPage displays a sample of the Arial font in the Preview pane.

3   In the Size list, click 4 (14 pt), and click OK.

The marquee text increases in size to 14 points.

Depending on the number of fonts that are installed on your computer, you might need to scroll down in the Font list to find the Arial font.

important

Points measure the height of text characters: there are 72 points per inch. Thus, 72-point type is one inch high, 12-point type is one-sixth of an inch high, and 14-point type is slightly less than one-fifth of an inch high.

Save

4   On the Standard toolbar, click the Save button.

FrontPage saves the home page.

5   Click the Preview tab at the bottom of the FrontPage window.

FrontPage displays a preview of the Web page. Notice that the marquee text scrolls from right to left.

Even though the Preview tab provides you with a quick look at a Web page's appearance, it doesn't show how the page will look when you load it in a Web browser. When you want an accurate view of a Web page, use the Preview In Browser button on the Standard toolbar to view the page in your default Web browser.

FP2000.10.1

Adding a Hit Counter to a Web Page

Ordinarily, it is impossible to determine the number of visitors to a Web site. With a **hit counter**, you solve that problem. A hit counter displays the number of visitors to a site since the hit counter was installed or reset. A hit counter can be a powerful marketing tool.

For example, Lakewood Mountains Resort could use a hit counter to gauge the success of its Web. A large number of visits might mean that the design has attracted a lot of interest to the site. Conversely, a small number of visits to the Web site might indicate that the design needs some work.

In this exercise, you add a hit counter to the Welcome page.

1 Click the Normal tab at the bottom of the FrontPage window.

2 Click at the end of the line *Call 1-800-555-1212 today!,* and press Enter.

The insertion point moves to a new line below the phone number.

3 On the Formatting toolbar, click the Font Size down arrow, and click 3 (12pt).

FrontPage will apply a 12-point text size to any text that is typed in this line.

4 Type **You are visitor number**, and press the Spacebar.

A caption is inserted for the hit counter.

5 On the Insert menu, point to Component, and click Hit Counter.

FrontPage displays the Hit Counter Properties dialog box.

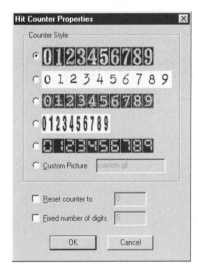

6 Click the third counter style from the top, select the Fixed Number Of Digits check box, and then click OK.

FrontPage inserts the hit counter at the selected location.

7 On the Standard toolbar, click the Save button.

FrontPage saves your changes.

important

To ensure that some components, such as the hit counter, work properly, make sure the Web is published to a server that supports the FrontPage Server Extensions.

Including One Web Page Inside Another

The Include Page component inserts a Web page inside another page. It can help you save time and space when creating a Web. If there is information that you want to appear on every page of a Web, such as a copyright notice or contact information, you can create one page that contains that information and include the page in all other pages instead of the Web to avoid having to type the information on every page.

In this exercise, you include the Copyright page inside the Lakewood Mountains Resort Welcome page.

1   Scroll down the Welcome page, if necessary, and click the line below the horizontal line at the bottom of the Web page.

FrontPage moves the insertion point to the bottom of the Web page.

2   On the Insert menu, point to Component, and click Include Page.

FrontPage displays the Include Page Properties dialog box.

3   Click the Browse button, and in the file list, click Copyrigh.htm (the Copyright Web page).

4   Click OK twice.

The dialog boxes close and the Copyright page is inserted at the bottom of the Welcome page.

5   If necessary, scroll down to view the included Web page.

The included page contains copyright information, an e-mail hyperlink, and the Site Created With Microsoft FrontPage logo.

Save

6   On the Standard toolbar, click the Save button.

FrontPage saves your changes.

Creating a Style

Themes are just one way that you can customize the appearance of your Web pages. Another way is to use **styles** and **style sheets**. A style is a set of characteristics (such as size, spacing, and color) that you apply to a Web page element, such as a heading. Style sheets are a collection of styles that you apply to an entire page.

Elements such as headings and text have a default appearance that depends partly on the visitor's Web browser and partly on the fonts installed on the visitor's computer. A style sheet is a collection of styles that you apply to an entire page, all Web pages, or selected pages in your Web.

You'll sometimes hear the terms **cascading style sheet (CSS)** or **external style sheet** used to refer to style sheets. These terms mean the same thing. A style sheet allows you to create formats for an entire page and then link the style sheet to all or selected pages in your Web to provide a uniform appearance for multiple Web pages.

In this exercise, you create a header style for a Web page in the Lakewood Mountains Resort Web.

1   In the Folder List, double-click the file Reasons.htm.

FrontPage displays the Reasons page.

2   On the Format menu, click Style.

FrontPage displays the Style dialog box.

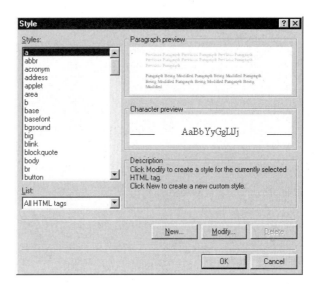

3   In the Styles list, scroll down, click H1, and then click Modify.

The Modify Style dialog box appears.

4   Click Format, and click Font on the Format menu.

The Font dialog box appears.

5   Click the Color down arrow, click the Blue square, and then click OK twice.

FrontPage creates an H1 style and sets the text color to blue. The Style dialog box reappears.

6   Click the List down arrow, and click All HTML Tags.

FrontPage redisplays the full list of Web page styles.

7   Click H2, and click the Modify button.

8   Click Format, and click Font on the Format menu.

FrontPage displays the Font dialog box.

9   Click the Color down arrow, click the Red square, select the All Caps check box, and then click OK three times.

The dialog boxes close, and FrontPage displays the style changes. Notice that the Heading 1 text is now blue, and the Heading 2 text is red and all uppercase.

FP2000.7.5

Using the Format Painter

Styling objects on a Web page can become repetitive, but it doesn't have to be. For example, if you decide to change the font style of all the hyperlinks in a Web (and you are not using a theme on the Web), you would have to select each text hyperlink and select the new font style for that hyperlink. However, say you have already created a style, or formatted text, that you want to use for another element of a Web site. FrontPage makes it easy to copy a style or format from one element to another.

With the **Format Painter**, you can copy formatting from selected text and apply it to other text. If you select characters to copy, the formatting applied to the individual characters is copied. If you select a paragraph (the selection includes the paragraph mark), the paragraph's style and character formatting are copied.

In this exercise you use the Format Painter to change the formatting of text on a Web page.

1   In the Folder List, double-click the file Welcome.htm.

FrontPage displays the Welcome page.

2   Select the phone number text.

Format Painter

3   Click the Format Painter button, and select the address text.

FrontPage instantly applies the formatting of the phone number to the address text.

Save

4   On the Standard toolbar, click the Save button.

> ## tip
> To copy the selected formatting to several locations, double-click the Format Painter button. Click the button again when you are finished formatting text to turn off the Format Painter.

Lesson Wrap-Up

This lesson covered how to apply a theme to an individual Web page, how to apply a theme to an entire Web, and how to modify and delete a theme. It also covered how to add, customize, and modify marquees; how to add a hit counter; how to place one Web page inside another page; how to create a style; and how to use the Format Painter.

If you are continuing to the next lesson:

● On the File menu, click Close Web. If FrontPage prompts you to save changes, click Yes.

FrontPage saves any changes and closes the Lesson04 Web.

If you are not continuing to other lessons:

Close

● Click the Close button in the top-right corner of the FrontPage window. If FrontPage prompts you to save changes, click Yes.

FrontPage saves any changes, closes the Web, and then quits.

Lesson Glossary

cascading style sheet (CSS) *See* style sheets.

components Ready-to-use programs, such as hit counters or marquees, that are activated when a visitor displays a page containing a component in his or her browser.

external style sheet *See* style sheets.

Format Painter A tool that allows you to copy formatting from the selected paragraph or text and apply it to other text.

hit counter A component that counts and displays the number of visitors to a Web since the hit counter was installed or reset.

marquee A design element that moves text across the screen when the Web page is displayed in a visitor's Web browser.

styles Sets of characteristics (such as size, spacing, and color) that can be applied to Web page elements, such as headings.

style sheets Collections of styles that you apply to entire Web pages.

theme A unified set of design elements, such as backgrounds and graphics, that you apply to Web pages to give them a consistent appearance.

Quick Quiz

1 How do you include one Web Page inside another?

2 Why must you be careful when using marquees?

3 Can you apply a background image to a Web page without using a theme?

4 How do you apply a FrontPage theme to a single page?

5 How do you apply a theme to an entire Web?

Putting It All Together

Exercise 1: Open the Lesson04 Web and select a theme for it. Apply that theme to the entire Web so that it has a bright color scheme and a consistent style or "look" for text, hyperlinks, buttons, banners, and other Web page elements.

Exercise 2: Add a marquee to the top of the home page welcoming visitors to the Lakewood Mountains Resort. Modify the marquee's appearance so that the font is 18 points and bold. Create a hit counter at the bottom of the page using the style of your choice.

LESSON 5

Formatting Web Pages

After completing this lesson, you will be able to:

✔ *Create and format a bulleted list.*

✔ *Create and format a numbered list.*

✔ *Insert a Microsoft Word document on a Web page.*

✔ *Insert a table on a Web page.*

✔ *Select and merge table cells.*

✔ *Delete table rows or columns.*

✔ *Insert and format text in a table cell.*

✔ *Format a table.*

Adding style to Web pages is not the only way to enhance a Web site. To make it easy for visitors to find information, you should also format the text in a logical manner. Microsoft FrontPage offers many ways to format a Web page. For example, if you have a lot of plain text on a Web page, organizing it in groups of bulleted lists helps make it more readable.

In this lesson, you will learn how to create and format bulleted and numbered lists. You will also learn how to create and format tables on Web pages, insert a Microsoft Word document on a Web page, and add and format a table on a Web page.

Sample files for the lesson

To complete the procedures in this lesson, you will need to create a new Web based on the files in the Lesson05 folder in the FrontPage Core Practice folder that is located on your hard disk. You will use this Web for all the exercises in Lesson 5.

If your hard disk uses a letter other than C, substitute the appropriate drive letter in place of C.

For the complete steps on importing a Web, see the "Using the CD-ROM" section at the beginning of this book or refer to the Lesson 1 section "Creating and Importing Webs."

1 On the File menu, point to New, and click Web.

2 Click the Import Web Wizard icon.

3 In the Specify The Location Of The New Web box, delete the default text and type **C:\My Webs\Lesson05**.

4 Click OK to continue.

Creating and Formatting a Bulleted List

You can organize content with two kinds of lists: bulleted and numbered. When you want a list to stand out, but you are not concerned with how the list is ordered, use a **bulleted list**. For example, you want to list Lakewood Mountains Resort's special programs for kids, but you do not want to number the activities in a specific order. A bulleted list will help the text stand out so that visitors can easily find the programs that appeal to their specific needs.

In this exercise, you create a bulleted list that describes hotel services and activities for kids.

1   In the Folder List, double-click the file Special_programs_for_kids.htm.

FrontPage opens the Web page in Page view.

2   Click the line below the heading.

Bullets

3   On the Formatting toolbar, click the Bullets button.

FrontPage inserts a bullet.

4   Type **State-certified daycare for toddlers**, and press Enter.

FrontPage creates the first bullet item and moves the insertion point down to the next line, adding a bullet.

5   Type **Junior lifesaving classes at the pool for ages 12-15**, and press Enter.

FrontPage creates the second bullet item and moves insertion point moves down to the next line, adding a bullet.

Bullets

6   On the Formatting toolbar, click the Bullets button.

FrontPage removes the bulleted list format from the bottom line.

You can also create your own list styles. On the Format menu, click Styles, click the New button, and then specify the attributes that you want for the style.

tip

To change a bulleted list to another list style, right-click one of the bullets, click List Properties, click the Other tab, click the list style that you want, and then click OK. You can change the bulleted list to a numbered list, definition list, directory list, or menu list.

7   Right-click one of the bullets in the list, and click List Properties on the shortcut menu.

FrontPage displays the List Properties dialog box with a variety of bullet styles.

8   Click the bottom-right sample box, which displays a square bullet style, and click OK.

FrontPage changes the bullet style to square bullets.

Save

9   On the Standard toolbar, click the Save button.

FrontPage saves your changes.

> ## tip
> To change the style of only one item in a list, right-click the item that you want to change, and click List Item Properties on the shortcut menu. In the dialog box, make the desired changes, and click OK.

Creating and Formatting a Numbered List

A **numbered list** usually indicates a sequence of events or is used to order items by importance. For example, you could use a numbered list to create an outline or to list an agenda. In the Lakewood Mountains Resort Web site, you decide to use a numbered list to display the directions to the resort.

In general, use bullets to indicate multiple options or alternatives. Use numbered lists for activities or instructions that are performed in sequence.

In this exercise, you create a numbered list of directions to Lakewood Mountains Resort.

1   In the Folder List, double-click the file Directions_to_lakewood.htm.

FrontPage displays the Web page in Page view.

2   Click the line below the heading,

Numbering

3   On the Formatting toolbar, click the Numbering button.

FrontPage inserts the number 1.

4   Type **Take the highway up from Santa Barbara**, and press Enter.

FrontPage creates the first list item and moves the insertion point down to the next line, adding the number 2.

5   Type **Turn left at the scarecrow**, and press Enter.

FrontPage creates the second list item and moves the insertion point down to the next line, adding the number 3.

6   Type **Go two miles, and you're here!**, and press Enter.

FrontPage creates the last list item and moves the insertion point down to the next line, adding the number 4.

Numbering

7   On the Formatting toolbar, click the Numbering button.

FrontPage removes the numbered list format from the bottom line.

> ## tip
> To continue a numbered list after intervening non-numbered text, first create the numbered list as directed in this exercise, and then right-click the first list item after the non-numbered text. On the shortcut menu, click List Properties, type the desired starting number for the continued list in the Start At box, and then click OK.

8   Right-click one of the numbers in the list, and click List Properties on the shortcut menu.

FrontPage displays the List Properties dialog box. Various numbering styles are shown.

Type a number in the Start At box when you want the numbered list to begin with a number other than 1.

9   Click the bottom-right sample box, which displays a lowercase Roman numeral numbering style, and click OK.

FrontPage changes the numbering style to lowercase Roman numerals.

Save

10   On the Standard toolbar, click the Save button.

FrontPage saves your changes.

tip

To change a numbered list to another style of list, right-click one of the numbers, click List Properties, click the Other tab, click the list style that you want, and then click OK. You can change the numbered list to a bulleted list, definition list, directory list, or menu list.

FP2000.5.2

Inserting a Microsoft Word Document on a Web Page

Using material that is already prepared saves you time when creating a Web. It also allows you to use the work of others who want to contribute to the Web without needing to retype all their work. When you use a Word document as the source file, you don't need to convert it to HTML. FrontPage automatically performs the conversion for you.

In this exercise, you insert a Microsoft Word document on the Location page of the Lakewood Mountains Resort Web.

New Page

1   On the Standard toolbar, click the New Page button.

FrontPage dispalys a new, blank Web page in Page view.

2   On the Insert menu, click File.

3   Navigate to the Extras folder in the FrontPage Core Practice folder on your hard disk.

4   Click the Files Of Type down arrow, and click All Files.

5   Click the Location file, and click Open.

    FrontPage inserts the contents of the file on the Web page.

Save

6   On the Standard toolbar, click the Save button.

    FrontPage saves your changes.

FP2000.9.1

Inserting a Table on a Web Page

Many Web pages present data in single-column format. They might add a bit of variety by left-aligning, right-aligning, or centering text or graphic elements, but their Web page elements are still displayed one after another down the page—not side by side.

In addition to its more conventional use of presenting information in a row-and-column format, a **table** lets you position elements side by side on a Web page. For example, you could use a table to display a photo and explanatory text side by side. You've planned several pages in the Lakewood Mountains Resort Web site that will benefit from using tables.

In this exercise, you insert a table on the On the Town Web page and specify the table size.

1   In the Folder List, double-click the file On_the_town.htm.

    FrontPage displays the Web page in Page view.

2   Click the line below the explanatory paragraph.

3   On the Table menu, point to Insert, and click Table.

    FrontPage displays the Insert Table dialog box.

> The In Percent option sizes the width of a table as a percentage of the user's browser window. You can gain more control over table size by clicking the In Pixels option and specifying the width in pixels. If you do this, you should strive to keep your table width small enough to fit within smaller monitors.

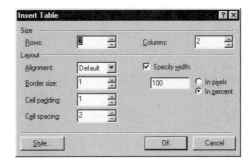

4   In the Rows box, delete the default value of 2, type **3**, and then click OK.

    FrontPage inserts a table with three rows and two columns.

FP2000.9.3

tip

Another way to create a table is to draw it using the mouse. To draw a table on a Web page, click Draw Table oin the Table menu, drag the mouse to form the outline of the table, drag the mouse to draw each row and column line, and then press Esc.

Notice on the menu that you can also use the Draw Table command to manually draw table rows and columns according to your desired dimensions.

5   On the Table menu, point to Insert, and click Rows Or Columns.

The Insert Rows Or Columns dialog box appears.

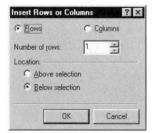

6   Double-click the Number Of Rows box, type **2**, and then click OK.

FrontPage inserts two rows at the bottom of the table.

FP2000.9.5

Selecting and Merging Table Cells

You can easily adapt a table to meet your needs. Sometimes the original format of the table does not work. For example, in a heading cell, it is useful to have the text run across the length of the table rather than be contained in a smaller space. Selecting the top row of cells and merging them into one cell solves your problem.

In this exercise, you merge two cells into one.

1   Click in the top-left cell in the table, and drag the mouse pointer from the top-left cell to the top-right cell.

The top row of cells is selected.

2   On the Table menu, click Merge Cells.

The two top cells are merged into one cell.

3   On the Standard toolbar, click the Save button.

Save

Deleting Table Rows or Columns

FP2000.9.2

When you are updating a Web, you might need to add or delete rows or columns from a table. Your design might change or you might need to alter the table's appearance. FrontPage makes the task quick and easy to perform.

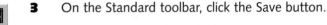

In this exercise, you delete a row from a table.

1   Select the entire bottom row of the table.

2   On the Table menu, click Delete Cells.

The row is deleted from the table.

Save

3   On the Standard toolbar, click the Save button.

Inserting and Formatting Text in a Table Cell

When you add text into table cells, you have quite a bit of control over the way the text is displayed in cells. Of course, you can format text just as you normally would (bold font, italic font, font style, font size, and so on). You can also use the Cell Properties dialog box to change the alignment of text within cells, along with other cell attributes.

In this exercise, you insert text into a table cell and format the cell contents by changing text alignment and font attributes.

1   Click in the right cell in the middle row of the table, and type **Visit the original Erewhon power plant, which generated electricity for miners during the California gold rush.**

FrontPage inserts the text into the table cell.

2   Press Tab twice, and type **Visit the Erewhon harbor, where fishing boats go out to sea.**

FrontPage moves the insertion point to the bottom-right table cell and inserts the text into the cell.

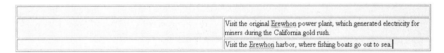

3   Select the two cells containing text.

4 Right-click the selected area, and click Cell Properties on the shortcut menu.

FrontPage displays the Cell Properties dialog box.

Select the Use Background Picture check box to insert a photo or other graphic as the background for the selected cells. To insert a background picture for an entire table, use the Table Properties dialog box.

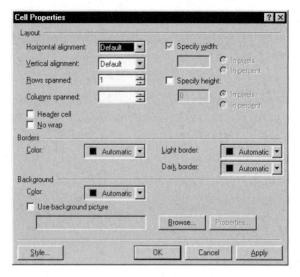

5 Click the Horizontal Alignment down arrow, click Right, and click OK.

The text is right-aligned within the cell.

6 Right-click the selected area again, and click Font on the short-cut menu.

FrontPage displays the Font dialog box.

Click the Character Spacing tab to create additional text effects. For instance, you can expand the spacing between characters (useful for creating eye-catching headings), and you can create superscript and subscript text by raising or lowering text on a line.

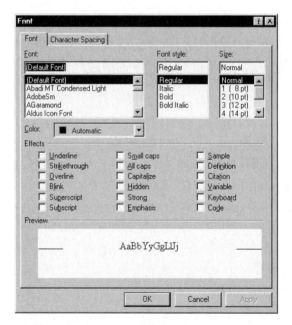

7 Click Arial in the Font list, click Bold Italic in the Font Style list, and click OK.

FrontPage changes the font and style of the text in the selected cells.

	Visit the original *Erewhon* power plant, which generated electricity for miners during the California gold rush.
	Visit the *Erewhon* harbor, where fishing boats go out to sea.

Save

8 On the Standard toolbar, click the Save button.

FrontPage saves your changes.

FP2000.9.4

Formatting a Table

After you create a table, you should customize it to fit your presentation needs. For example, you can customize the table's column width and row height to control how text flows in a cell. You can also customize a table's border, changing the border's size and appearance to make the table more readable.

In this exercise, you format a table by changing its column width, row height, and border style to better accommodate the material that you entered in previous exercises.

1 Position the mouse pointer over the horizontal border under the text *gold rush*.

The mouse pointer changes to a vertical double arrow.

2 Drag the border down approximately ½ inch.

FrontPage makes the row taller and vertically centers the text.

3 Position the mouse pointer over the vertical border in the center of the table.

The mouse pointer changes to a horizontal double arrow.

4 Drag the border approximately ¼ inch to the left.

FrontPage resizes the table columns.

5 Right-click one of the table borders, and on the shortcut menu, click Table Properties.

FrontPage displays the Table Properties dialog box.

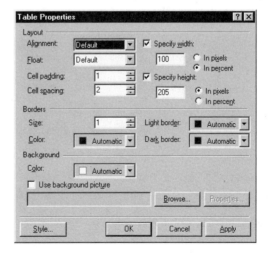

6 Click in the Size box in the Borders section, delete the default value of 1, type **0**, and then click OK.

FrontPage makes the table borders invisible. The table's border position is represented by dashed lines when the page is displayed using the Normal tab in Page view.

Save

7 On the Standard toolbar, click the Save button.

FrontPage saves your changes.

8 Click the Preview tab.

FrontPage displays a preview of the table. Notice that the borders are invisible.

Lesson Wrap-Up

This lesson covered how to create and format bulleted lists and numbered lists, how to work with numbered lists, how to insert a Microsoft Word document on a Web page, and how to work with tables.

If you are continuing to the next lesson:

● On the File menu, click Close. If FrontPage prompts you to save changes, click Yes.

FrontPage saves any changes and closes the Lesson05 Web.

If you are not continuing to other lessons:

Close

● Click the Close button in the top-right corner of the FrontPage window. If FrontPage prompts you to save changes, click Yes.

FrontPage saves any changes, closes the Lesson05 Web, and then quits.

Lesson Glossary

bulleted list A list of items in an unspecified order in which each item is preceded by a symbol.

numbered list A sequential list of items in which each item is preceded by a number. FrontPage 2000 supports automatic numbering for a new numbered list and automatic renumbering when a numbered list is edited.

table An arrangement of information in columns and rows that can be sized and formatted as a unit.

Quick Quiz

1 How do you create a bulleted list?

2 How do you insert a Microsoft Word document on a Web page?

3 How do you insert a table on a Web page?

4 How do you merge table cells?

5 How do you delete table cells?

Putting It All Together

Exercise 1: Create a new page. On the new page, create a numbered list with the following text:

1. Visit the Lakewood Mountains Resort Web site.
2. Make a reservation.
3. Visit Lakewood Mountains Resort.

Create a bulleted list with the following text:

- Relaxation
- Rest
- More Relaxation

Exercise 2: Insert a two-row-by-two-column table onto the page you created in the previous exercise. In the top-left table cell, type **Main building**. In the top-right table cell, type **Swimming Pool**. Select the two cells in the top row. Change the cell properties to center the cell contents horizontally, and save the page.

Adding Multimedia to Web Pages

After completing this lesson, you will be able to:

✔ *Insert a photo on a Web page.*

✔ *Explore the Clip Art Gallery.*

✔ *Insert clip art on a Web page.*

✔ *Insert an image in a table and create a thumbnail.*

✔ *Move image files to the Images folder.*

✔ *Edit a Web page image.*

✔ *Add text over an image.*

✔ *Add a background sound to a Web page.*

✔ *Add a video clip to a Web page.*

✔ *Link a video clip to a Web page.*

Although you can use a Web site to display a lot of information, to really impress visitors, you need to make the site interesting and pleasurable. A state-of-the-art Web site makes use of images, sound, and video to create a well-rounded presentation. Microsoft FrontPage provides you with the tools necessary to easily add **multimedia** elements to a Web.

In this lesson, you will learn how to insert photos and clip art images on Web pages. You will also learn how to insert images in table cells on a Web page and how to create thumbnails of those images. You will then learn how to add a background sound and a video clip to a Web page.

Sample files for the lesson ⇨

To complete the procedures in this lesson, you will need to create a new Web based on the files in the Lesson06 folder in the FrontPage Core Practice folder that is located on your hard disk. You will use this Web for all the exercises in Lesson 6.

If your hard disk uses a letter other than C, substitute the appropriate drive letter in place of C.

For the complete steps on importing a Web, see the "Using the CD-ROM" section at the beginning of this book, or refer to the Lesson 1 section "Creating and Importing Webs."

1 On the File menu, point to New, and click Web.

2 Click the Import Web Wizard icon.

3 In the Specify The Location Of The New Web box, delete the default text, and type **C:\My Webs\Lesson06**.

4 Click OK to continue.

FP2000.6.1

Inserting a Photo on a Web Page

You can use three kinds of image formats on Web pages: **GIF** (Graphics Interchange Format), **JPEG** (Joint Photographic Experts Group), and **PNG** (Portable Network Graphics). GIF, JPEG, and PNG files compress an image, allowing a smaller file size than other formats. The small file size allows photos to be downloaded quickly to a Web site visitor's computer.

The purpose of the Lakewood Mountains Resort Web is to promote the resort to Web visitors so that they'll want to vacation at the resort. To raise interest, you need to make the Web as exciting as possible. When you add photos of the resort to the Web, you provide a way for visitors to view the beauty and elegance of the resort.

In this exercise, you insert a photo of the resort's main building on the Lakewood Mountains Resort Welcome01 page.

1   In the Folder List, double-click the file Welcome01.htm.

FrontPage displays the Welcome page in Page view.

2   Click the blank line below the text *Lakewood Mountains Resort* and above the resort's address.

The insertion point is centered on the line.

You can also use this submenu to insert a video file. For best results in all Web browsers, it's a good idea to insert only videos that are in the AVI format (files that have the .avi extension).

3   On the Insert menu, point to Picture, and click From File.

FrontPage displays the Picture dialog box.

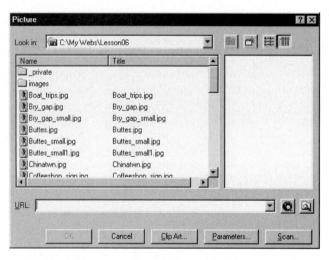

4   In the file list, click Main_building.jpg, and click OK.

FrontPage inserts the image at the location that you selected. The image is so large that it pushes the resort's address and phone number off the bottom of the window.

Save

5   On the Standard toolbar, click the Save button.

FrontPage saves your changes.

> **tip**
> By reducing the size of image files, you reduce the time it takes visitors to download them. Apart from reducing the size of the image itself, another good way to shrink file size is to use an image-editing program such as Jasc Software's Paint Shop Pro or Microsoft PhotoDraw to reduce the number of colors in the image.

Exploring the Clip Art Gallery

Generally, **clip art** images are ready-made electronic illustrations that you insert into a document. The **Clip Art Gallery** also includes ready-made sounds and motion clips that you can use on a Web page. Use the Clip Art Gallery when you want to easily add buttons, cartoons, images, and backgrounds to a Web.

In this exercise, you explore the Clip Art Gallery.

1   In the Folder List, double-click the file Sights01.htm.

FrontPage displays the Web page.

2   On the Insert menu, point to Picture, and click Clip Art.

FrontPage displays the Clip Art Gallery window. On the Pictures tab, you can select clip art images to insert on Web pages.

The Search For Clips box in the Clip Art Gallery dialog box provides a fast and easy way to locate an image for use in a Web.

3   Click the Sounds tab.

On the Sounds tab, you can select sound effects to insert on Web pages.

4   Click the Motion Clips tab.

On the Motion Clips tab, you can select motion clips and animated GIF files to insert on Web pages.

An animated GIF file is actually a series of images that are displayed sequentially to give the appearance of motion.

5   In the Categories pane, click the Academic icon.

FrontPage displays the motion clips available in this category.

6   Click one of the motion clip pictures.

FrontPage displays the shortcut menu for the motion clip.

Play Clip

7   On the shortcut menu, click the Play Clip icon.

FrontPage plays the motion clip in the GIF Player window.

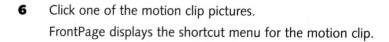

Close

8   Click the Close button in the top-right corner of the GIF Player window.

FrontPage closes the GIF Player window.

Back

9   On the Clip Art Gallery toolbar, click the Back button.

FrontPage redisplays the Motion Clips tab of the Clip Art Gallery window.

Close

10   Click the Close button in the top-right corner of the Clip Art Gallery window.

FrontPage closes the window.

> When you download images from the Internet for use on your Web site, always check for copyright or permission information to make sure the way you will use the image complies with the owner's wishes.

tip

To download additional clip art images, sounds, and motion clips from the Internet, on the Clip Art Gallery toolbar, click Clips Online. FrontPage connects to the Microsoft Clip Gallery Live Web site from which you can download additional clip art images, sounds, and motion clips for your Web pages. You can also download clip art, sounds, and motion clip files from newsgroups on the Internet such as *alt.binaries.sounds.midi*.

Inserting Clip Art on a Web Page

Now that you have a good idea of the variety of clip art that the Clip Art Gallery offers, it is time to put some of the files to use. You decide that you want to add a graphical element to the Sights01 Web page that will give visitors a visual representation of the page's contents. You start by browsing the Clip Art Gallery to find a suitable image.

In this exercise, you search for an arrow graphic from the Clip Art Gallery and insert the graphic on the Sights01 Web page.

1   On the Sights01 Web page, click the blank line below the heading and above the table.

FrontPage moves the insertion point to the line below the heading.

2   On the Insert menu, point to Picture, and click Clip Art.

FrontPage displays the Clip Art Gallery window.

3   Click in the Search For Clips box, type **arrow**, and then press Enter.

FrontPage searches the Clip Art Gallery for arrow images and displays the search results on the Pictures tab.

4   Click one of the arrow images.

FrontPage displays the shortcut menu for the clip art image.

Insert Clip

5 On the shortcut menu, click the Insert Clip icon.

FrontPage inserts the image at the selected location on the Web page and closes the Clip Art Gallery window.

Save

6 On the Standard toolbar, click the Save button, and click OK in the Save Embedded Files dialog box.

FrontPage saves the Web page with your changes.

tip

You can make a hyperlink out of almost any image on a Web page, including clip art images. To create a hyperlink from a clip art image, right-click the image, and click Hyperlink on the shortcut menu. In the Create Hyperlink dialog box, browse to the file that will be the link target, click the file, and then click OK.

Inserting Images in Tables and Creating Thumbnails

One way to position images on a Web page is to use a table. A table provides an easy way to lay out text and graphics. By taking advantage of the ability to format specific cells in a table, you can make graphics a valuable part of any Web site. An especially helpful FrontPage feature creates thumbnails. A **thumbnail** is a small version of an image that downloads very quickly. You should use a thumbnail when you have a very large image that you want to display. Generally, the larger an image, the longer it takes for the image to load in a visitor's Web browser. When you create a thumbnail, you give a visitor the option to view the larger image, rather than having to wait for the image to load with the rest of the page. To view the full-sized image, a visitor clicks the thumbnail, which then loads the full-sized image on a separate page.

You do not need to use a table to display a thumbnail. The table in this exercise is used to position the thumbnail in a specific place on the page.

In this exercise, you arrange images on a Web page by inserting them in table cells. You then shrink those images by converting them to thumbnails that link to the full-sized images.

1 In the Folder List, double-click the file Sights02.htm.

FrontPage opens the Web page in Page view.

You can also click the Web Browser button (to the right of the URL box) to browse to, select, and insert a picture from a publicly available Web page. If you do this, make sure you observe any copyright restrictions.

2   Click the top-left cell in the table. On the Insert menu, point to Picture, and click From File.

FrontPage displays the Picture dialog box.

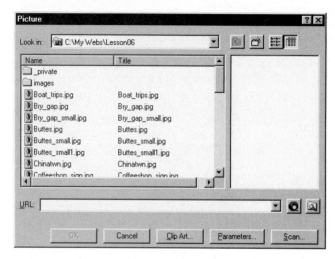

3   In the file list, click Bry_gap.jpg, and click OK.

FrontPage inserts the image into the table cell. Notice that the image does not fit well in the table cell.

4   Click the image in the table cell.

FrontPage displays the Pictures toolbar along the bottom of the screen.

Auto Thumbnail

5   On the Pictures toolbar, click the Auto Thumbnail button.

FrontPage converts the table image into a much smaller thumbnail that is a hyperlink to the full-sized image.

6   Click the middle cell of the top row.

7   On the Insert menu, point to Picture, click From File, click Shore.jpg, and then click OK.

FrontPage inserts an image into the middle cell of the row.

8   Click the image in the middle cell, and on the Pictures toolbar, click the Auto Thumbnail button.

FrontPage creates a thumbnail image and links it to the full-size image.

Save

9   On the Standard toolbar, click the Save button, and click OK in the Save Embedded Files dialog box.

FrontPage saves your changes.

Preview In Browser

10   On the Standard toolbar, click the Preview In Browser button.

FrontPage displays the Sights02 page in your default Web browser.

11   Click the Shore thumbnail.

The Web browser loads the full-sized image.

Close

12   Click the Close button in the top-right corner of the Web browser window.

The Web browser closes and FrontPage appears.

Moving Image Files to the Images Folder

When you create a Web, FrontPage automatically creates a folder called Images within the main Web folder. If the Web has a large number of images, moving all image files to the Images folder makes the image files easier to find.

In this exercise, you move image files from the main folder of the Lesson06 Web to its Images folder and observe how FrontPage updates the hyperlink to each image.

1 On the Views bar, click the Folders icon.

FrontPage displays a list of all files in the Lesson06 Web.

2 Click the Type column heading at the top of the file list.

FrontPage displays the files in alphabetical order by type.

3 In the file list, click Boat_trips.jpg. Hold down the Shift key, and then press the Down arrow key until all the JPEG image files are selected.

4 Drag the selected files to the Images folder in the Folder List.

> You do not need to place images in the Images folder for the Web to work. The Images folder is provided to easily organize Web files.

FrontPage moves all the JPEG image files to the Images folder and updates all hyperlinks between the Web pages and the JPEG files to reflect the files' new location.

5 In the file list, click FrontPageLogo.gif, hold down the Ctrl key, and click any other GIF files.

The GIF image files are selected.

> The JPEG (Joint Photographic Experts Group) graphic format was designed for color photographs and supports a larger number of colors and increased color resolution than the older GIF (Graphic Interchange Format).

6 Drag the GIF image files to the Images folder in the Folder List.

FrontPage moves all the GIF image files to the Images folder and updates the hyperlinks.

7 On the Views bar, click the Page icon, and double-click the file Sights03.htm in the Folder List.

FrontPage displays the Web page in Page view.

8 Right-click the picture in the top-left table cell, and on the shortcut menu that appears, click Hyperlink Properties.

FrontPage displays the Edit Hyperlink dialog box. Notice that the hyperlink's target (in the URL box) has been updated and is in the Images folder.

9 Click Cancel in the Edit Hyperlinks dialog box.

FrontPage closes the Edit Hyperlinks dialog box.

FP2000.8.1

Editing Images on Web Pages

Putting an image on a Web page is easy, but frequently the image is too large or too small to fit comfortably on the page. Making the size of an image manageable is an important part of designing a Web. You want the image to fit snugly into a visitor's browser window. Additionally, you should make sure that the image file is not so large that it causes a visitor's browser to load the page too slowly.

Moreover, some visitors set up their Web browsers to download Web pages without embedded images. Doing so makes the pages download more quickly but leaves gaps where images would otherwise appear. Using FrontPage, you can specify **image alternative text** when images are not downloaded. Instead of the image, Web page visitors see the alternative text description at the page location where the image would ordinarily appear.

In this exercise, you resize the hotel image on the Welcome02 Web page to make it better fit the page. You then specify an alternative text description for the hotel image.

1   In the Folder List, double-click the file Welcome02.htm.

FrontPage displays the Welcome Web page in Page view. The hotel image is so large that it pushes the address and phone number off the bottom of the window.

2   Click the hotel image, and scroll to the lower-right corner of the image.

A small square (a resize handle) appears at the corner of the image.

3   Move the mouse pointer over the resize handle.

The mouse pointer changes into a diagonal double-arrow.

You can also use the resize handles at the top, bottom, or sides of an image to resize it. However, when you use resize handles other than the ones in the corners of the image, the original porportions of the image will not be retained.

4   Drag the mouse pointer upward and to the left to shrink the image.

FrontPage resizes the hotel image, retaining the original proportions.

5   Right-click the hotel image, and click Picture Properties on the Shortcut menu.

FrontPage displays the Picture Properties dialog box.

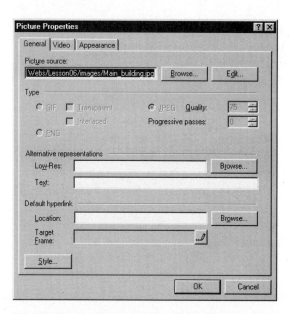

6   Click in the Text box in the Alternative Representations section, type **Lakewood Mountains Resort main building**, and then click OK.

FrontPage inserts the text that will be displayed if a Web site visitor's browser does not display Web page images.

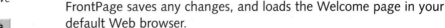

Save

7 On the Standard toolbar, click the Save button, and click the Preview In Browser button.

FrontPage saves any changes, and loads the Welcome page in your default Web browser.

Preview In Browser

8 Position the mouse pointer over the hotel image.

The alternate text appears next to the mouse pointer.

Close

9 Click the Close button in the top-right corner of the Web browser.

The Web browser closes and FrontPage appears.

FP2000.8.2

Adding Text over an Image

Adding text over an image is an easy way to customize the images that you use. Text helps a visitor to identify the image without having to place a label at the bottom of the image, where it is sometimes overlooked.

In this exercise, you add descriptive text to the hotel image on the Welcome Web page.

Text

1 Click the hotel image, and click the Text button on the Pictures toolbar at the bottom of the FrontPage window.

A dialog box appears, telling you the image will be converted to GIF format.

2 Click OK.

3 Using the handles at the edges of the text box, resize and drag the text box so that it covers the lower portion of the image.

4 Type **Lakewood Mountains Resort**.

The text is added to the picture.

5 On the Formatting toolbar, click the Font Size down arrow, and click 5 (18pt).

FrontPage resizes the text.

6 On the Formatting toolbar, click the Font Color down arrow, and click the White square.

FrontPage changes the text color to white. The image should look similar to the following.

Save

7 On the Standard toolbar, click the Save button, and click OK.

Adding a Background Sound to a Web Page

Most Web page content is informative, but there is more to the Web experience than just getting information. You want the Lakewood Mountains Resort Web site to be a pleasant place to visit. One way to make the site interesting is to add a background sound to the home page. This background sound plays as long as the home page is displayed in a Web browser.

important

If you use these steps to insert a sound file on a Web page, the sound file will play when the page is loaded in Microsoft's Internet Explorer Web browser, but not when the page is loaded into Netscape's Navigator Web browser.

In this exercise, you add a background sound to a Web page and preview the sound in your Web browser.

1   In the Folder List, double-click the file Welcome03.htm.

FrontPage displays the Welcome page in Page view.

2   Right-click any blank area of the page, and click Page Properties on the Shortcut menu.

FrontPage displays the Page Properties dialog box.

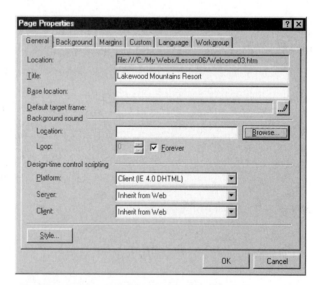

3   Click Browse.

FrontPage displays the Background Sound dialog box.

4   Click Tolizt01.mid, and click OK twice.

FrontPage inserts the MIDI (Musical Instrument Digital Interface) file as a background sound that plays as long as the page is displayed in a visitor's Web browser.

Depending on a visitor's Internet connection speed, the sound clip might take awhile to load in a visitor's Web browser.

Save

Preview In Browser

Close

5   On the Standard toolbar, click the Save button, and click the Preview In Browser button.

FrontPage saves the page and displays it in your default Web browser. If you are using Internet Explorer, the background sound plays automatically.

6   Click the Close button in the top-right corner of the Web browser window.

The Web browser closes and FrontPage appears.

To hear the background sound, you must have a sound card and speakers installed on your computer.

tip

By default, a background sound continues to play as long as the Web page is displayed in a visitor's Web browser. However, you can specify that the sound play a certain number of times and then stop. In the Page Properties dialog box, clear the Forever check box. In the Loop box, enter the number of times that the background sound should be repeated, and click OK.

Adding a Video Clip to a Web Page

Using a video clip on a Web page can really enhance the way the Web page presents information. When Web site visitors load a page with an embedded motion clip, the video automatically plays both motion and sound. For example, you might include a video clip on the Lakewood Mountains Resort Web site that gives visitors a guided tour of the resort. The video clip would allow Web visitors to experience the resort rather than just view static pictures of it.

In this exercise, you insert a motion clip on the Pc_help01 Web page and preview the video in your Web browser.

Depending on visitors' Internet connection speed, the video clip might take awhile to load on their Web browser.

1   In the Folder List, double-click the file Pc_help01.htm.

FrontPage displays the Web page in Page view.

2   Click the blank line just below the page text. On the Insert menu, point to Picture, and click Video.

FrontPage displays the Video dialog box as shown on the next page.

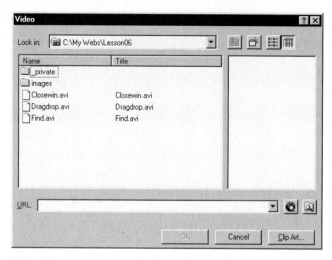

3   Click Closewin.avi, and click OK.

FrontPage inserts the motion clip directly on the Web page. When a Web site visitor displays the page, the video will play once.

Save

4   On the Standard toolbar, click the Save button, and then click the Preview In Browser button.

FrontPage saves the page and displays it in your Web browser. The motion clip plays automatically.

Preview In Browser

5   Click the Close button in the top-right corner of the Web browser window.

The Web browser closes and FrontPage appears.

☒

Close

Linking to a Video Clip

It is not necessary to insert a video clip directly on a Web page. Linking to a clip is just as effective and reduces the size of the Web page file. Creating a link to a motion clip reduces the time it takes the page to load in a visitor's browser.

In this exercise, you create a hyperlink to the Dragdrop.avi video clip rather than inserting the file directly on a Web page.

> When you provide a link to a video clip (rather than inserting a clip on a Web page), you reduce the time it takes for the page to load in a visitor's browser.

1   In the Folder List, double-click the file Pc_help03.htm.

FrontPage displays the Web page in Page view.

2   Select the text *How to drag and drop.*

3   Right-click the selected text, and click Hyperlink on the shortcut menu.

FrontPage displays the Create Hyperlink dialog box.

4 In the file list, click Dragdrop.avi, and click OK.

FrontPage inserts the hyperlink.

Save

5 On the Standard toolbar, click the Save button, and then click the Preview In Browser button.

FrontPage saves the Web page and displays it in your Web browser.

Preview In Browser

6 Click the How To Drag And Drop hyperlink.

Windows Media Player opens and plays the motion clip.

7 Close Windows Media Player and the Web browser.

FrontPage is redisplayed.

Lesson Wrap-Up

This lesson covered how to insert a photo on a Web page, how to use the Clip Art Gallery, how to create image thumbnails, how to move image files to different folders, how to resize an image, how to use alternative text for an image, how to add text over an image, and how to use sound and video to enhance a Web site.

If you are continuing to the next lesson:

● On the File menu, click Close Web. If FrontPage prompts you to save changes, click Yes.

FrontPage saves any changes and closes the Lesson06 Web.

If you are not continuing to other lessons:

Close

● Click the Close button in the top-right corner of the FrontPage window. If FrontPage prompts you to save changes, click Yes.

FrontPage saves any changes, closes the Web, and then quits.

Lesson Glossary

clip art Ready-made electronic illustrations that can be quickly and easily inserted into a document.

Clip Art Gallery A collection of images that is included with your installation of FrontPage and is located on your hard disk.

GIF An acronym for Graphic Interchange Format. GIF is a file format used for compressing and storing images.

image alternative text Text that is displayed when a visitor's browser does not display images.

JPEG An acronym for Joint Photographic Experts Group, JPEG (also called JPG) is a file format that provides more powerful color resolution and compression capabilities than GIF.

multimedia The integrated presentation of text, graphics, video, and sound on a computer.

PNG An acronym for Portable Networks Graphics, PNG is a file format that provides additional capabilities over the JPEG format, including automatic detection of transmission errors and color-matching correction to provide a true color representation on different monitors.

thumbnail A miniature display of a graphic image that downloads very quickly because of its small size.

Quick Quiz

1 How do you insert a photo on a Web page?

2 How do you search the Clip Art Gallery for an image?

3 Why do you need alternative text for an image?

4 How do you create a thumbnail?

5 What are the three image file types that can be used on a Web page?

Putting It All Together

Exercise 1: Using the Search For Clips box, browse the Clip Art Gallery to find the image of a man resting on the earth.

Exercise 2: Create a table with two rows and two columns. Add any two images to the left two cells in the table, and then create a thumbnail of each image. Add text over each image to give it a descriptive title. Insert the following text into the right two cells of the table: **Click the image to view the full-size image.**

LESSON 7

Updating a Web

After completing this lesson, you will be able to:

✔ *Check spelling on an entire Web.*

✔ *Check spelling on a single Web page.*

✔ *Change a file name in Folders view.*

✔ *Publish a Web locally.*

✔ *Rename a Web.*

✔ *Update a Web.*

As you create and edit pages in a FrontPage Web, you might find it necessary or helpful to perform some additional housekeeping tasks to ensure that your Web is as accurate and as current as possible. For example, you might want to check the spelling on all pages in your Web or on just the page you are editing. You might also decide to rename the Web to give it a more descriptive name for other Web developers who access and edit pages in the Web.

In this lesson, you will learn how to check the spelling in a Web prior to publishing it. You'll learn how to publish a Web locally to make a backup copy of your Web files; how to rename a Web; and how to update a published Web on your hard disk.

Sample files for the lesson

To complete the procedures in this lesson, you will need to create a new Web based on the files in the Lesson07 folder in the FrontPage Core Practice folder that is located on your hard disk. You will use this Web for all the exercises in Lesson 7.

1   On the File menu, point to New, and click Web.

2   Click the Import Web Wizard icon.

3   In the Specify The Location Of The New Web box, delete the default text, and type **C:\My Webs\Lesson07**.

4   Click OK to continue.

> If your hard disk uses a letter other than C, substitute the appropriate drive letter in place of C.
>
> For the complete steps on importing a Web, see the "Using the CD-ROM" section at the beginning of this book or refer to the Lesson 1 section "Creating and Importing Webs."

Checking Spelling on an Entire Web

At Impact Public Relations, the marketing copywriters have a poster on the wall that reads: "No wun spels perfecly all the thyme." No matter how carefully you type information on the Web pages for Lakewood Mountains Resort, at least a few spelling errors are inevitable.

Before you publish a Web, you need to ensure that the text on all Web pages is free of errors. Careless text errors in a Web can make you and your organization appear unprofessional. Although FrontPage can't identify or help you correct grammatical errors, it can identify misspellings on Web pages. You can use the **Spelling** feature to locate potential misspellings and to correct spelling errors.

When the Spelling feature identifies a potentially misspelled word, it displays a list of suggestions. You can use this list to select the correct spelling for a misspelled word. Because proper names and many technical terms are not included in FrontPage's spelling dictionary, they are often marked by the spelling checker as being potentially incorrect, even though they are spelled correctly. To keep the original spelling of a word, you click Ignore. To keep the original spelling of the word throughout the page or the Web, you click Ignore All.

By default, the spelling checker checks words as you type them on a page, and marks any words (with a jagged red underline) that are not in the spelling dictionary. You can correct any suspect words as soon as you notice that the spelling checker has underlined them, or you can choose to check the spelling on all Web pages at one time.

When you check spelling in an entire Web, FrontPage displays a list of pages with misspelled words. The advantage of using the list is that it helps you to see all the pages in a Web that contain misspellings. FrontPage marks the pages with a red bullet. You can double-click a page in this list to identify and correct each misspelling.

important

Performing an automated spelling check is certainly beneficial, but it is no substitute for proofreading Web pages. For example, in the marketing copywriters' adage, the word *time* is misspelled as *thyme*. FrontPage's spelling checker would not have caught that error because *thyme* is a real word; however, it is the wrong word in this particular context.

In this exercise, you check and correct spelling of text on all pages in the Lakewood Mountains Resort Web.

1   On the Views bar, click the Navigation icon.

The Lesson07 Web appears in Navigation view.

If you click Spelling on the Tools menu when you are in Page view, FrontPage will check spelling on only the currently open page.

2   On the Tools menu, click Spelling.

FrontPage displays the Spelling dialog box. The Entire Web option is selected.

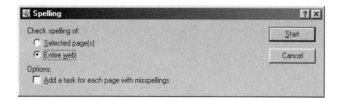

3   Click Start.

FrontPage displays a list of pages with spelling errors. In each row, FrontPage lists the page number, the number of errors on that page, and the misspelled words.

4   In the Spelling dialog box's Page column, double-click the file Dining.htm.

FrontPage displays the Dining page in Page view. The first word that FrontPage identifies as being potentially misspelled appears in the Spelling dialog box.

If you want to add a word to the FrontPage spelling dictionary, click the Add button in the Spelling dialog box when the word you want to add is displayed.

5   In the Suggestions list, click cuisine, and click Change. (On this page, only one word is misspelled. If other words on had been misspelled, after you clicked Change, the spelling checker would display the next word on the page that is potentially misspelled.)

FrontPage corrects the word and displays the Continue With Next Document? dialog box.

If you frequently use a proper noun (such as a person's name, the name of a company, or the name of a city) that you know FrontPage will flag as a misspelling, click the Add button to add the word to the dictionary. Doing so will prevent FrontPage from marking the word as being misspelled from this point forward.

6   Click Next Document.

FrontPage saves your changes to the Dining page, closes the Dining page, and displays the next Web page with spelling errors.

7   Click Cancel three times to close the dialog boxes without correcting the spelling errors.

FrontPage ends the spelling check.

You will learn more about tasks in Lesson 8, "Managing and Enhancing a Web."

tip
If you want to locate spelling errors now, but you do not want to correct spelling until a later time, in the Spelling dialog box, select the Add A Task For Each Page With Misspellings check box, and click Start. FrontPage compiles a list of pages with spelling errors and adds them as tasks in Tasks view. When you decide to correct spelling, just click the Tasks icon on the Views bar, and double-click pages in Tasks view that are flagged as having misspelled words.

FP2000.12.1

Checking Spelling on a Single Web Page

When you make changes throughout a Web, you should check the spelling of the entire Web. However, when you update only one page, you can save time by opening that page in Page view and checking the spelling on just the single page.

In this exercise, you check and correct spelling on the History and Personnel page of the Lakewood Mountains Resort Web.

1   In the Folder List, double-click the file History.htm.

FrontPage displays the History and Personnel page in Page view.

2   On the Tools menu, click Spelling.

FrontPage displays the Spelling dialog box. FrontPage displays the word *Bromo* in the Spelling dialog box because the word does not appear in the spelling dictionary. In this case, you know that *Bromo* is a proper name and is spelled correctly.

> Click the Change All button to change all instances of a misspelled word throughout a page or on all pages in a Web.

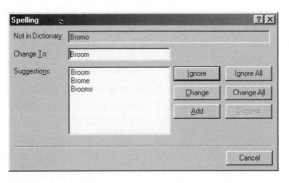

3   Click Ignore.

FrontPage displays the next apparent misspelling. In this case, the word *hotel* is misspelled as *hotl*.

4   In the Suggestions list, click hotel, and click Change.

FrontPage corrects the word on the Web page and displays the next misspelling.

5   In the Suggestions list, click problem, and click Change.

FrontPage corrects the word on the Web page and displays the next misspelling. You know that *M.I.T.* is short for *Massachusetts Institute of Technology*, so the word is not misspelled.

6   Click Ignore, and click Ignore for any other spelling errors on the page.

FrontPage displays a message box stating that the spelling check is complete.

7   Click OK, and click the Close button in the top-right corner of the History and Personnel page. When you are prompted to save your changes, click Yes.

FrontPage saves your changes and closes the History and Personnel Web page.

tip

If you need to see a word in context on the Web page to determine if it is misspelled, drag the Spelling dialog box to one side of the screen.

FP2000.12.2

Changing a File Name in Folders View

Occasionally, you might need to rename a file in a Web to better fit the naming convention of the Web. For example, you've decided to add information about room service to the dining page of the Lakewood Mountains Resort Web. You should change the file name for the page to better describe the new content of the page. The procedure is straightforward, and if the page contains any hyperlinks, FrontPage automatically repairs and updates any hyperlinks to or from the renamed file. This is an important benefit that FrontPage offers because it saves you from the lengthly process of updating hyperlinks manually. It also ensures that your hyperlinks remain accurate.

In this exercise, you rename the file Dining.htm *Food.htm*, and you rename the file Location.jpg *Mountains.jpg*.

1   In the Folder List, right-click the file Dining.htm.

A shortcut menu appears.

2   Click Rename.

3   Type **Food.htm**, and press Enter.

FrontPage asks if you want to update these pages so that the hyperlinks are not broken.

You can test a hyperlink in Normal view by pressing Ctrl and clicking the hyperlink.

4   Click Yes.

FrontPage renames the file and updates the hyperlinks for that page.

5   In the Folder List, right-click the file Location.jpg, and click Rename on the shortcut menu.

6   Type **Mountains.jpg**, press Enter, and then click Yes.

FrontPage renames the file and updates the hyperlinks for the image.

7   In the Folder List, double-click the file Index.htm.

8   Click the Preview tab.

FrontPage displays a preview of the Index page.

9   Click the *Dining* hyperlink on the Index page.

FrontPage loads the Dining page that you renamed *Food.htm*.

10   Click the *Location* hyperlink.

FrontPage loads the Location page.

Publishing a Web Locally

You have worked hard to create a good looking Web using FrontPage. You've previewed the Web pages in your default browser, and you've checked the Web for spelling errors. You are confident that the Web will meet the needs of your client, but you want view the Web as a finished product before you publish it to a Web server.

Publishing a Web to a Web server is covered in the *Microsoft FrontPage 2000 Step by Step Courseware Expert Skills* course.

FrontPage allows you to **publish** a Web locally, to your hard disk, so that you can view a working copy of the Web. A locally published Web also allows you to view all of the elements and components of the Web so that you can check that they are working properly. For instance, you must publish a Web to view a hit counter on a Web page. You must also publish a Web to test any forms you have created.

A locally published Web can also serve as a backup copy to the Web after you publish it to a server. If you make changes to the working copy of the Web (the one you publish to a server) and then want to undo those changes, you can refer to the original (locally published) copy of the Web.

In this exercise, you publish a copy of the Lakewood Mountains Resort Web to your hard disk.

1   On the File menu, click Publish Web.

FrontPage displays the Publish Web dialog box.

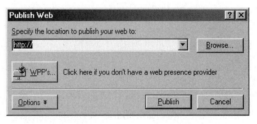

If your hard disk uses a letter other than C, substitute the appropriate drive letter in place of C.

2   In the Specify The Location To Publish Your Web To box, type **C:\My Webs\Copy of Lesson07 Web**, and click Publish.

FrontPage publishes a copy of the Web to your hard disk and displays a message box confirming that the publication succeeded.

3   Click Done.

FrontPage closes the message and dialog boxes.

Renaming a Web

FrontPage assigns a Web the same name as the folder in which the Web is kept, whether it is on a local hard disk or on a remote Web server. For example, the current Web that you've been working on in this lesson is named Lesson07. You can assign a more descriptive name to the Web such as *Lakewood* or *Lakewood Mtn Resorts* so that you can more easily recognize the Web's content.

In this exercise, you rename the Lesson07 Web *Lakewood Mountains Resort*.

important

The steps for renaming a Web are the same whether you rename a Web on your local hard disk or on a remote Web server. However, depending on your access permissions, you might not be able to rename a Web on a Web server. Check with your system administrator or your Internet service provider if you need help.

1 On the Tools menu, click Web Settings.

FrontPage displays the Web Settings dialog box.

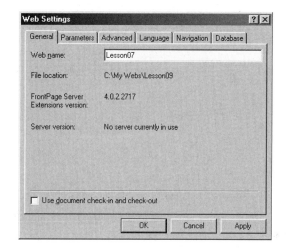

You can use the Navigation tab to change the text labels that appear on navigation bar buttons.

2 In the Web Name box, delete the default name, type **Lakewood Mountains Resort**, and then click OK.

FrontPage renames the Web *Lakewood Mountains Resort*.

Updating a Web

After a Web has been created, or even while it's still under construction, the Web files are typically stored on a Web server or on a network server (such as a Microsoft Windows NT server or a Microsoft Windows 2000 server) so that other users can access the Web. Even if other users only view Web files rather than make changes to them, the Web files need to be stored in a location that all users can access. A server is typically the best resource for this purpose.

However, you might want to make changes and modifications to Web files without disturbing visitors to the Web. To do so, you could import the Web to your own hard disk, make changes as necessary, and then **update** the original Web on the server.

(continued)

continued

Updating a Web

When you use FrontPage to update a Web, you can instruct FrontPage to update only those pages on your hard disk version of the Web that are different from identically named pages on the server.

In other words, FrontPage updates the Web server with your changes and leaves all unaffected pages in their previous condition. Updating a Web is a quick way to publish only pages that you've edited, instead of having to republish the entire Web site.

The following steps explain how to update a Web stored on your hard disk to a server location that already contains a previous version of the Web.

> You can also mark individual pages so that they are not published, even if you have made changes to the pages. To do so, in the Folder List, right-click the name of a page, and click Properties. Click the Workgroup tab, and select the Exclude This File When Publishing The Rest Of The Web check box. This technique is useful if you want to publish your Web but are still working on one or more pages that are not ready to be published.

1   On the File menu, click Publish Web.

FrontPage displays the Publish Web dialog box.

2   In the Options section of the dialog box, click the Publish Changed Pages Only option.

When this option is selected, FrontPage uploads pages to the server only if they were changed since they were originally published on the server.

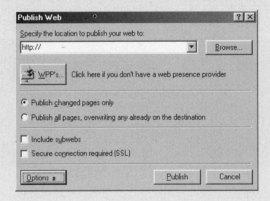

3   In the Specify The Location To Publish Your Web To box, type the URL for a server on the Internet or type a path to a folder stored on a network server.

4   Click Publish.

FrontPage updates the Web page files on your hard disk and displays an alert box confirming that the publication succeeded.

5   Click Done.

6   On the File menu, click Close Web.

FrontPage closes the Web.

Lesson Wrap-Up

This lesson covered how to check spelling on a single Web page, how to check spelling on an entire Web, how to publish a Web locally, how to change a file name while maintaining its hyperlinks, and how to rename a Web.

If you are continuing to the next lesson:

● On the File menu, click Close Web. If FrontPage prompts you to save changes, click Yes.

FrontPage saves any changes and closes the Lesson07 Web.

If you are not continuing to other lessons:

Close

● Click the Close button in the top-right corner of the FrontPage window. If FrontPage prompts you to save changes, click Yes.

FrontPage saves any changes, closes the Web, and then exits.

Lesson Glossary

publish To make a Web you've prepared available for visitors to see.

Spelling A FrontPage feature that marks potentially misspelled words in a Web page as you type them and allows you to check for and correct misspellings in all pages in a Web.

update On a Web server, the process of publishing changed Web pages by replacing outdated, existing pages stored on a Web server.

Quick Quiz

1   If the FrontPage spelling checker identifies a word as misspelled, but you know that the word is spelled correctly, how can you prevent the spelling checker from identifying this word as misspelled on other Web pages?

2   How do you check spelling on a single Web page?

3   Why is it a good idea to publish a Web locally before you publish it to a Web server?

4   How do you rename a Web page?

5   How do you update hyperlinks after you've renamed a Web or a Web page?

6   How do you check spelling on all pages in a Web?

Putting It All Together

Exercise 1: Open the Lesson05 Web, and check the spelling on the entire Web. Proofread it to look for words that are spelled correctly but are used in the wrong context, such as *thyme* rather than *time*.

Exercise 2: Rename the Lesson05 Web *Lakewood Mtns Resort*. Rename the On_the_town.htm file *Erewhon.htm*, rename the Roomres.htm file *Reservations.htm*, and rename the Character.htm file *Aboutus.htm*. Publish the Web to your hard disk, and preview the Web in your default Web browser.

LESSON 8

Managing and Enhancing a Web

After completing this lesson, you will be able to:

✔ *View reports on the status of a Web.*

✔ *Change Reports view options.*

✔ *Create and assign tasks.*

✔ *Perform a task.*

✔ *View and sort tasks.*

✔ *Create a table of contents.*

✔ *Animate text with dynamic HTML.*

✔ *Create page transition effects.*

✔ *Create a search page.*

You've learned how to publish and maintain a Web, but the task of managing it might seem overwhelming compared to the ease with which it can be created. How do you coordinate the work that your staff is performing to create the site? How do you keep track of all the updates that you need to do once the site has been published? And how do you gather information about a Web so that you can decide if you want to enhance its design? The answer, of course, is that you use Microsoft FrontPage. FrontPage includes valuable tools for managing and enhancing a Web.

In this lesson, you will learn how to view reports on various aspects of a Web. You'll change Reports view options to account for different styles and needs of management. You'll also learn how to create and assign tasks for updating a Web. Finally, you'll learn how to further enhance a Web by animating page text, creating page transition effects, and adding a search page to a Web.

Sample files for the lesson

If your hard disk uses a letter other than C, substitute the appropriate drive letter in place of C.

For the complete steps on importing a Web, see the "Using the CD-ROM" section at the beginning of this book or refer to the Lesson 1 section "Creating and Importing Webs."

To complete the procedures in this lesson, you will need to create a new Web based on the files in the Lesson08 folder in the FrontPage Core Practice folder that is located on your hard disk. You will use this Web for all the exercises in Lesson 8.

1   On the File menu, point to New, and click Web.

2   Click the Import Web Wizard icon.

3   In the Specify The Location Of The New Web box, delete the default text, type **C:\My Webs\Lesson08**.

4   Click OK to continue.

FP2000.11.1

Using Reports View

The first step in updating or enhancing a Web is to find out what you need to update or enhance. Reports view provides a quick look into the operation of a Web, which can make the job of managing a Web easier. You can display information about different aspects of a Web, such as which hyperlinks are broken, which pages load more slowly than others, and so on.

The advantage of using Reports view is that it allows you to see what needs to be accomplished before you start the process of updating a Web. For example, if you want to double-check that all the hyperlinks are complete, you would first view a report listing all missing hyperlinks in the Web. If you want to improve the Web's performance, you would first view a report that lists estimated loading times for all the pages in the Web.

In this exercise, you use Reports view to see reports on different aspects of the Lakewood Mountains Resort Web.

1   On the Views bar, click the Reports icon.

FrontPage displays the Site Summary report, which lists the categories of reports available, the number of files covered in each category, the total size of files in each category, and a description of each category.

Close

tip

If a floating toolbar appears over the Reports window, close it by clicking the Close button in its top-right corner.

> You can widen any column in the Site Summary by dragging the right edge of the gray column heading. For instance, you can widen the *Name* column to see the complete names for all report items.

2   In the Site Summary report, double-click the Broken Hyperlinks line.

FrontPage displays a list of possible broken hyperlinks. In this case, three possible broken hyperlinks are listed: two lead from the Lakewood home page (Index.htm) to Web pages that were renamed. The third hyperlink is not broken, but because it leads to a Web page on the Internet, FrontPage cannot verify that it is not broken.

3   Right-click the Index1.htm line, and click Edit Hyperlink on the shortcut menu.

FrontPage displays the Edit Hyperlink dialog box.

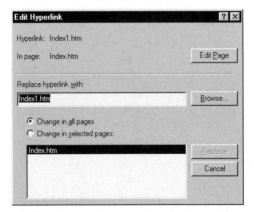

4   Click Edit Page.

FrontPage displays the page containing the broken hyperlink. Notice that the broken hyperlink (Use Frames) is already selected.

5   Right-click the broken hyperlink, and click Hyperlink Properties on the shortcut menu.

FrontPage displays the Edit Hyperlink dialog box.

6   In the file list, click Index01.htm, and click OK.

FrontPage repairs the broken hyperlink.

Save

7   On the Standard toolbar, click the Save button, click the Close button in the top-right corner of the page, and then click the Reports icon on the Views bar.

Close

FrontPage displays the Broken Hyperlinks report. Two possible broken hyperlinks remain.

You can also click the Publish Status command on the submenu that appears in step 8 to view a report that indicates which pages have been published and which pages have not yet been published.

8   On the View menu, point to Reports, and click Site Summary.

FrontPage redisplays the Site Summary report.

Changing Reports View Options

You can alter Reports view options to control what pages FrontPage considers recent, old, or slow to download. For example, the Lakewood Mountains Resort Web does not contain much content that needs to be updated frequently. You might need to update rate information, or activity information once every season, but it doesn't make much sense to spend time updating the Web every day or even once a week. In such cases, you would set the Older Files Are More Than option to 60 days so that only FrontPage reports files over 60 days old as old files.

You can also use Reports view options to specify the **Assume Connection Speed for a Web.** The assume connection speed is the speed that FrontPage uses to determine whether pages will load quickly in a visitor's browser. For example, if you set an assume connection speed of 28.8, FrontPage will generate a slow to download report for all pages that will load slowly on a browser that has a maximum connection speed of 28.8 KBps (kilobytes per second).

In this exercise, you change Report view options by specifying which files are considered recent and which pages are considered slow to download. You also view the assumed speed of your Internet connection.

1   On the Tools menu, click Options.

FrontPage displays the Options dialog box.

2   Click the Reports View tab.

3   Delete the default text in the "Recent" Files Are Less Than box, and type **15**.

In Reports view, FrontPage will list files added in the previous 14 days as recently added files.

4   In the "Slow Pages" Take At Least box, click the up arrow five times to increase the value to 35.

In Reports view, FrontPage will list files that take at least 35 seconds to download as slow pages.

5   Click the Assume Connection Speed Of down arrow, and view the list of options. Click the down arrow again to close the list without changing the value, and click OK.

FrontPage applies your changes.

The new DSL (Digital Subscriber Line) connection type is not represented in the list. A DSL connection is faster than ISDN but slower than T1. If you want to assume a connection speed for DSL, select ISDN speed in the list.

Reports Created by FrontPage

Reports provide information about various aspects of Webs that you created using FrontPage. The following table describes the reports that you can view and their content. To view a report, on the View menu, point to Reports, and then click the report you want to see.

Report	Content
Site Summary	All available reports on the Web.
All Files	All files in the Web, with file name, title, folder location, size, file type, date last modified, and author.
Pictures	All picture files in the Web.
Unlinked Files	All files not linked to the Web's home page.
Linked Files	All files linked to the Web's home page.

(continued)

continued

Reports Created by FrontPage

Report	Content
Slow Pages	All files that take longer to load than the time specified on the Reports View tab of the Options dialog box.
Older Files	All files older than the number of days specified on the Reports View tab of the Options dialog box.
Recently Added Files	All files added within the number of days specified on the Reports View tab of the Options dialog box.
Hyperlinks	All hyperlinks in the Web.
Unverified Hyperlinks	All hyperlinks whose target files have not been verified.
Broken Hyperlinks	All hyperlinks whose target files cannot be found.
External Hyperlinks	All hyperlinks with target files outside the Web.
Internal Hyperlinks	All hyperlinks with target files inside the Web.
Component Errors	All FrontPage components in the Web that are not functioning properly.
Uncompleted Tasks	All uncompleted tasks in Tasks view.
Unused Themes	All themes contained in the current Web but not used.

Files that are marked as Slow Pages will change if the Assume Connection Speed Of Entry is changed in the Options dialog box.

Creating and Assigning Tasks

Once you have used FrontPage's Reports view to identify the areas that you need to update or enhance in a Web, use Tasks view to track what's been done, by whom, and what still needs to be done. You can also create new tasks and edit previously created tasks in Tasks view.

For example, you might assign tasks to different members of your Web design team at Impact Public Relations. You could assign one person to work on updating the Recreation page content and another person to refine the Dining page so that it loads more quickly.

In this exercise, you create tasks and assign them to members of your Web design team.

1   On the Views bar, click the Tasks icon.

FrontPage displays the Tasks list. The list is empty because you haven't created any tasks yet.

You can also create a new task by right-clicking in the right pane and clicking New Task.

2   On the File menu, point to New, and click Task.

FrontPage displays the New Task dialog box. The Assigned To box already has your user name in it because you created the Web.

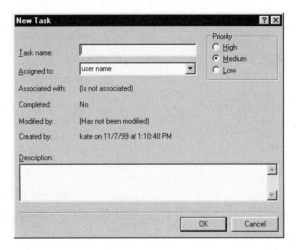

The actual Assigned To name is the name that was entered when FrontPage was installed. Additional names will appear in the list if the Workgroup tab of the Properties dialog box has been used to add other users for any files stored in the Web.

3   Click in the Task Name box, and type **Call Lakewood re: search page**.

4   Click in the Assigned To box, delete the default text, and type **Jim**.

You've assigned the task to Jim, a member of your project team.

5   Click in the Description box, type **Get verbal approval from resort manager to create a search page**, and then click OK.

FrontPage creates the new task and displays it in the list of tasks. The entry shows that the task is not yet started and displays the rest of the task information in summary form.

6   On the Views bar, click the Reports icon, and double-click the line for Broken Hyperlinks.

FrontPage displays a list of the Web's broken hyperlinks. If you completed the exercise "Using Reports View," earlier in this lesson, Reports view lists only two possibly broken hyperlinks. If you did not complete the exercise, Reports view lists three possibly broken hyperlinks.

7   Right-click the line for the Index03a.htm broken hyperlink, and click Add Task on the shortcut menu.

FrontPage displays the New Task dialog box. The task name (Fix broken hyperlink) and description (Broken URL is Index03a.htm) are already filled in for you.

8   Click OK.

FrontPage creates a new task. In the Status column, the line for the broken hyperlink now reads Added Task.

Performing a Task

The value of using FrontPage to create and assign tasks is that FrontPage allows you to see which tasks are completed and which tasks still need to be performed. There are two ways to mark a task as completed. When you perform a task on a Web page, FrontPage asks if you want to mark the task as completed. You can also manually mark a task as completed. You would do so if you had completed a task not directly associated with a Web page. For example, you would manually mark the *call Lakewood re: search page task* as complete because the task does not require any changes to one of the Lakewood Mountains Resort Web pages.

In this exercise, you repair a broken hyperlink and mark the task as completed.

You can also change the name of a task or reassign the task to a different person by right-clicking the task and clicking Edit Task.

1   On the Views bar, click the Tasks icon.

FrontPage displays the Web's list of tasks.

2   Double-click the Fix Broken Hyperlink task.

FrontPage displays the Task Details dialog box.

3   Click Start Task.

FrontPage displays the page containing the broken hyperlink in Page view. Notice that the broken hyperlink (No Frames) is already selected.

4   Right-click the broken hyperlink, and click Hyperlink Properties on the shortcut menu.

FrontPage displays the Edit Hyperlink dialog box.

5   Scroll down the file list, click Index02.htm, and then click OK.

FrontPage repairs the broken hyperlink.

Save

6   On the Standard toolbar, click the Save button.

FrontPage asks if you want to mark the task as completed.

Close

7   Click Yes, click the Close button in the top-right corner of the page, and then click the Tasks icon on the Views bar.

FrontPage displays the Tasks list. The Fix Broken Hyperlink task is now marked Completed.

8   Right-click the remaining task to be completed, Call Lakewood Mountains Resort, and click Mark As Completed on the shortcut menu.

FrontPage marks the task as completed (even though you did not actually complete it).

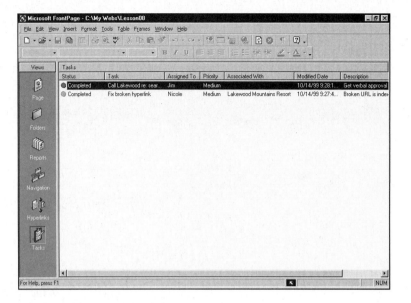

FP2000.13.2

Viewing and Sorting Tasks in Tasks View

Once you create and assign tasks, you need to know how to manage their performance. The FrontPage view of tasks helps you see who did what task and when they finished it. When you create a Web, FrontPage automatically builds a list of tasks. Sorting the tasks is as simple as clicking a column heading. You can sort tasks in the list of tasks by status (Not Started or Completed), by task name, by person, by priority, and by date modified.

In this exercise, you view and sort the tasks necessary for the Lakewood Mountains Resort Web.

1 Click the Assigned To column heading to sort the tasks alphabetically by the name of the task owner.

If the tasks are already listed alphabetically, their order won't change.

2 Click the Task column heading to sort the tasks alphabetically by task name.

Creating a Table of Contents

In Lesson 4, "Adding Style to Web Pages," you learned about FrontPage components. A component is a ready-to-use program that is activated when a visitor loads the page in his or her Web browser. The FrontPage Table of Contents is a component that you insert on a Web page to catalog a Web's contents. The advantage of using the Table of Contents component is that whenever you add a new page to a Web, the table of contents is updated automatically—unlike a standard hyperlinks menu, which you must update manually to add new hyperlinks or change old ones. The only disadvantage is that you have less control over what links are included in the Table of Contents than you do with a list of hyperlinks that you create manually.

In this exercise, you create a Table of Contents page and preview it in your Web browser.

New Page

1 On the Views bar, click the Page icon, and click the New Page button on the Standard toolbar.

FrontPage creates a new Web page and displays it in Page view.

2 On the Insert menu, point to Component, and click Table Of Contents.

FrontPage displays the Table Of Contents Properties dialog box.

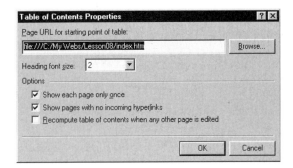

tip

Another way to create a table of contents is to use the Table Of Contents page template. Click the Page icon on the Views bar, point to New on the File menu, click Page, click the Table Of Contents template icon, and then click OK. The result is the same as if you had inserted a Table of Contents component on a blank page.

Select the Recompute Table Of Contents When Any Other Page Is Edited check box if you want to ensure that the Table of Contents is updated when you edit, delete, or add pages to your Web.

3 Select the Recompute Table Of Contents When Any Other Page Is Edited check box, and click OK.

FrontPage inserts a Table of Contents component on the Web page.

4 Right-click a blank area of the Web page, and click Page Properties on the shortcut menu.

FrontPage displays the Page Properties dialog box.

5 In the Title box, type **Table of Contents**, and click OK.

The page's descriptive title appears when you display the Web in Folders view or when a dialog box displays it in a file list.

6 On the File menu, click Save As.

FrontPage displays the Save As dialog box.

7 In the File Name box, type **TOC1**, and click Save.

FrontPage saves the Table of Contents page. Notice that TOC1.htm now appears in the Folder List.

Preview In Browser

8 On the Standard toolbar, click the Preview In Browser button.

FrontPage opens the page in your default Web browser and displays the table of contents for the Web site. When visitors click the links, their browser loads the corresponding pages in the Web.

Notice that two Lakewood Mountains Resort links appear—one for the frames version of the home page (Index01), and one for the no-frames version (Index02).

9   Click the Close button in the top-right corner of the Web browser.

The Web browser closes, and FrontPage reappears.

tip

If you create a home page that lets visitors select a frames or no-frames version of the Web, you can create a separate table of contents for each version. Right-click the Table of Contents component on the Web page, and click Table Of Contents Properties on the shortcut menu. In the Table Of Contents Properties dialog box, click Browse, select the top page of the associated branch in the Web hierarchy (for example, the top page of the frames version of the Web), and click OK. The table of contents includes only pages below the selected page in the Web hierarchy.

Animating Text with Dynamic HTML

The Lakewood Mountains Resort Web site is running smoothly. The resort managers are excited about the way you have presented the content, and they appreciate the frequency and accuracy with which you update the Web. Visits to the site have been increasing steadily, and visitors' comments have been overwhelmingly positive, but the resort staff wants you to wow visitors by making the whole site come alive. You decide to add some additional effects to make the Web more like an interactive slide show.

Text animation will not work in older browser versions that do not support dynamic HTML. However, even if you include text animation, visitors who use older browsers will still see the text, even though it won't be animated.

FrontPage makes it easy to create a **text animation effect**. First you decide when you want the animation to occur, and then you choose the animation effect. You can animate Web page text so that it spirals into position, drops onto the page one word or one letter at a time, swoops in from the left or right, or appears with many other surprising effects.

In this exercise, you animate text by using FrontPage's ready-to-use dynamic HTML features.

1   In the Folder List, double-click the file Dhtml01.htm.

FrontPage displays the Dhtml01.htm page in Page view.

2   Select the first line of text, and on the Format menu, click Dynamic HTML Effects.

FrontPage displays the floating DHTML Effects toolbar.

3   Click the On down arrow, and in the list, click Page Load.

The dynamic HTML effect will be activated when a visitor loads this page into a Web browser.

4   Click the Apply down arrow, and in the list, click Drop In By Word.

When the page loads in a Web browser, the text will seem to drop from above onto the page.

Remember that to see the effects, you need to save the page and then display it in your Web browser. Such effects are not shown in FrontPage.

5 Drag the DHTML Effects toolbar out of the way, if necessary, and select the second line of text.

6 On the DHTML Effects toolbar, click the On down arrow, and click Mouse Over. Click the Apply down arrow, and click Formatting.

7 Click the Choose Settings down arrow, and click Choose Font.

FrontPage displays the Font dialog box.

8 In the Font list, click Arial. In the Size box, type **18**. Click the Color down arrow, click the Red square, and click OK.

Close

9 Click the Close button in the top-right corner of the DHTML Effects toolbar. On the Standard toolbar, click the Save button.

FrontPage closes the Dynamic HTML toolbar and saves the Web page with your changes.

Save

10 On the Standard toolbar, click the Preview In Browser button.

FrontPage starts your default Web browser and loads the dynamic HTML page. As the page loads, the top line of text drops into place.

Preview In Browser

11 Move the mouse pointer over the second line of text.

The text font changes to Arial, the size increases to 18 points, and the text color changes to red.

12 Move the mouse pointer away from the text.

The text changes back to its original font, size, and color.

Close

13 Click the Close button in the top-right corner of the Web browser.

The Web browser closes and FrontPage reappears.

FP2000.10.2

Creating Transition Effects

A **page transition** is a ready-made DHTML effect that controls how one Web page loads or disappears when another page loads. You use page transitions to make a Web act more like a slide show. When you create a page transition, you can use circular or straight-line animations or make one page slide in from the left or right side over the previous page. For example, you should insert page transitions on the Lakewood Mountains Resort Web to provide movement from the home page to the Dining page, the home page to the Recreation page, and the home page to the Location page. The page transitions would sell the resort's atmosphere by simulating a slide show that visitors might watch after a vacation at Lakewood Mountains Resort.

In this exercise, you create special transition effects for a Web page.

1 In the Folder List, double-click the file Index.htm.

FrontPage displays the page in Page view.

2 On the Format menu, click Page Transition.

FrontPage displays the Page Transitions dialog box.

If FrontPage displays a message box warning you that the page transition effect requires a Web browser that supports dynamic HTML, such as Microsoft Internet Explorer 4.0 or later, click OK.

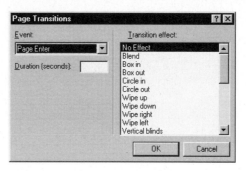

3   Click the Event down arrow, and click Page Exit in the list.

The page transition effect will occur when a visitor leaves the page.

4   In the Duration (Seconds) box, type **2**.

The page transition effect will last for two seconds.

5   In the Transition Effect list, click Vertical Blinds, and click OK.

The Vertical Blinds transition effect is selected.

Save

6   On the Standard toolbar, click the Save button, and click the Preview In Browser button.

FrontPage saves your changes, starts your default Web browser, and displays the selected Web page.

Preview In Browser

7   Click the Use Frames hyperlink.

As the new Web page loads, the old page disappears behind an effect that resembles opening vertical blinds on a window.

Close

8   Click the Close button in the top-right corner of the Web browser window.

The Web browser closes, and FrontPage reappears.

FP2000.10.4

Creating a Search Page

On a **search page**, Web site visitors type a key word or phrase that would probably appear on the pages they want to see and click a Submit button. Then the server then returns a list of all pages on the Web site that contain that word or phrase.

Setting up a search page is easy in FrontPage. You simply click the Page icon on the Views bar and create a new page using the Search Page template in the New dialog box. FrontPage creates a search page with boilerplate text that you can modify for your Web's specific needs. When visitors submit a search, a **search engine** looks for the relevant pages on the Web site.

important

To use a search page in FrontPage, you need to make sure that you publish the Web to a server that supports the FrontPage Server Extensions. When the Web is published to such a server, FrontPage creates an index based on all the text in the Web. When a visitor submits a search form, the server searches the index and displays a list of hyperlinks to pages that contain the search text.

In this exercise, you create a search page for the Lakewood Mountains Resort Web site.

1   On the File menu, point to New, and click Page.

FrontPage displays the New dialog box.

2   Scroll down on the General tab, click the Search Page icon, and click OK.

FrontPage creates a new page using the Search Page template.

Because a search page uses the text index that is created when you create or import a Web, searches will work in most browsers and browser versions.

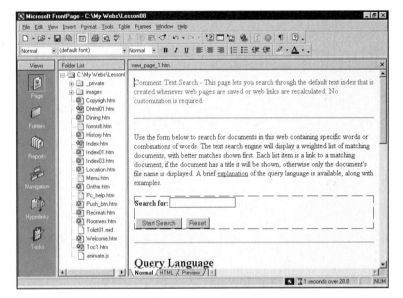

3   At the top of the page, delete the comment text, and click the Heading 1 style in the Style list on the Formatting toolbar.

Center

4   Type **Lakewood Mountains Resort**, hold down the Shift key and press Enter, type **Search Page**, and click the Center button on the Formatting toolbar.

FrontPage creates a page heading and centers it on the page.

5   Press Enter, and click the Center button on the Formatting toolbar.

FrontPage inserts a new line aligned on the left under the heading.

6   Type **This page enables you to search for activities and services offered at Lakewood Mountains Resort.**

7   On the File menu, click Save As.

FrontPage displays the Save As dialog box.

8   In the File Name box, type **Search01.htm**.

FrontPage enters Search01.htm as the file name for the new page.

9   Click Change. In the Set Page Title dialog box, type **Search this Web site** as the page title, and click OK. Click Save.

FrontPage changes the page title and saves the new search page.

Testing the Search Page

To test a search page in a browser, you need to first publish the Web. When you publish a Web—either to a Web server or to your own computer with the Microsoft Personal Web server installed—the search page is displayed as a normal Web page form.

Simply type the desired search word(s) in the Search For box, and click Start Search. The Web server returns a list of the pages on the Web that contain the search word(s). In the list, each item is a hyperlink to the corresponding page. Click each hyperlink to verify that the search page displays the desired pages.

Lesson Wrap-Up

This lesson covered how to view reports on various aspects of a FrontPage-based Web, how to change Reports view options, how to animate Web page text with dynamic HTML, how to create and assign tasks for updating or enhancing the Web, how to create a table of contents for a Web site, how to create page transition special effects, and how to create a search page.

If you are continuing to the next lesson:

● On the File menu, click Close Web. If FrontPage prompts you to save changes, click Yes.

   FrontPage saves your changes and closes the Lesson08 Web.

If you are not continuing to other lessons:

Close

● Click the Close button in the top-right corner of the FrontPage window. If FrontPage prompts you to save changes, click Yes.

   FrontPage saves any changes, closes the Web, and then exits.

Lesson Glossary

assume connection speed for a Web The speed that FrontPage uses to determine whether pages will load quickly in a visitor's browser.

DHTML (dynamic HTML) An extension of HTML (Hypertext Markup language) that provides greater control over the layout of Web pages and the ability to create special effects.

page transition A ready-made DHTML effect that controls how one Web page loads or disappears when another page loads.

search engine A program that searches a Web for a specific word or phrase and returns a list of all pages that contain the search item.

search page A page where Web site visitors type a word or phrase that they are looking for in the pages that they are viewing.

text animation effect A ready-made DHTML effect that controls how Web page text appears when the page is loaded.

Quick Quiz

1   How do you change Reports view options?

2   What are the column headings that you can use to sort tasks?

3   What does an Unverified Hyperlinks report display?

4   How do you modify Reports view to show pages that will take longer than 5 seconds to download on a 14.4-KBps connection?

5   How do you manually mark a task as completed?

Putting It All Together

Exercise 1: Using the Table of Contents page template, create a second table of contents page for the Lakewood Mountains Resort Web that displays the contents for the no-frames version of the Web.

Exercise 2: Using dynamic HTML effects, animate each of the Index01 hyperlinks so that they fly off the left of the page when clicked.

APPENDIX A

Features that Require the FrontPage Server Extensions

In an ideal situation, you develop a Web site in Microsoft FrontPage and publish it to a Web server that has the FrontPage Server Extensions installed. However, if you don't have access to a FrontPage-compliant Web server, some features that you create in FrontPage won't work.

Understanding FrontPage-Specific Features

There are two categories of features that require the FrontPage Server Extensions to work properly. The first category consists of run-time components. When Web pages are loaded into a browser, these components interact with the Web server. If the Web server isn't set up to work with FrontPage components, the components won't function properly.

Run-time Component	Explanation
Confirmation field	Confirms the data a user enters in a form field.
Default form handler	Sends form data to a Web page file.
Hit Counter component	Counts and displays the number of times a page has been viewed by Web site visitors.
Registration component	Registers Web site visitors to create a members-only Web site.
Scheduled Include Page component	Inserts one Web page in another Web page at a specified time.
Scheduled Picture component	Inserts an image on a Web page at a specified time.
Search component	Inserts a search form on a Web page.

The second category consists of components that depend on extra Web information that is stored by FrontPage—in particular, information about the Web hierarchy that you can create in Navigation view. These components won't work because the server doesn't store and provide that information as needed.

Navigational component	Explanation
Navigation bar	Displays hyperlinks in shared borders.
Page Banner component	Displays the page title at the top of the page.
Table of Contents component	Creates and displays a Web site table of contents.

Using Workarounds for FrontPage Components

Navigational components are the easiest components to replace with Web page workarounds.

Navigational component	Replace with
Navigation bars	Manually created hyperlinks.
Page Banner component	Text page heading (use Heading 1 style).
Table of Contents component	A page of hyperlinks in a menu frame.

Run-time components can often be replaced by components designed for the specific non-FrontPage Web server to which you're publishing the Web. For example, the popular GeoCities Web site has its own hit counter, guest book, and other components that you can download. You can then use FrontPage to incorporate these components into your Web pages and upload them (manually, of course) to the Web site.

APPENDIX B

Internet Service Providers that Support FrontPage

This appendix lists Internet service providers (ISPs) in North America that, at the time of publication, provide Web hosting services using the FrontPage Server Extensions. All the providers in this appendix have passed Microsoft's Server Extension installation and configuration tests (a requirement to be listed as a provider on the FrontPage Web site) and have registered with Microsoft. Neither Microsoft Press nor ActiveEducation endorses any of the providers listed in this appendix. These providers are listed solely as a service to individuals who have taken the *Microsoft FrontPage 2000 Step by Step Courseware* core skills or expert skills course or who have purchased this book and would like to publish their Webs to a FrontPage-compliant Web server located in their state, province, or territory.

To use this appendix, locate an ISP in your locale, enter the URL for the ISP in the Address bar of your Web browser, and press Enter to view more information about the ISP, including the types of Web hosting services that the ISP offers, setup and monthly hosting fees, and contact information to arrange hosting for your Web. Some ISPs periodically offer special deals for individuals and organizations that want to host a FrontPage-compliant Web, so you should visit all of the available providers in your locale to compare fees and special offers.

ISPs change ownership frequently, and some might not be in business at the time that you read this. Consequently the URLs for ISPs sometimes change or might no longer exist. For an updated listing of FrontPage-compliant ISPs, visit *www.microsoft.com/FrontPage*, and follow these steps:

1 Click the Internet Service Providers That Support FrontPage link.

2 Click the Search By Location (U.S./Canada Only) link.

3 Click the By State, Province, Or Territory down arrow, click the name of your state, province, or territory, and then click the Go button.

Note that the Microsoft FrontPage Web site changes frequently, so the precise steps to follow might differ when you visit the site.

If you live outside the U.S. or Canada, this site also includes a link that you can use to view information about International ISPs that support the FrontPage Server Extensions.

With most Web browsers, you do not need to enter the *http://* portion of the URL.

important

Some of the URLs in this appendix wrap to two lines. Make sure you do not enter any spaces in a URL, even if the appearance of a URL suggests a space. A valid URL cannot have a blank space. Also, enter hyphens in URLs just as you see them in this appendix. If you enter a Web address that has a line-ending hyphen and the URL does not work, try entering the URL without the hyphen that appears at the end of the line in this appendix.

ISP Name	Location	URL
Alabama		
Gulf Coast Network Systems, Inc.	Daphne	http://www.gulfnetsys.com
Alberta		
CYBERStream Inc.	Calgary	http://www.cyberstream.net/frontpage
ENVISIONIT Global IT Solutions	Sherwood Park	http://www.envisionit.ca/wpp/index.htm
TardisNet	Calgary	http://www.tardisnet.net/frontpage.htm
UCBIZ Internet Services Ltd	Edmonton	http://ucbiz.com/service_page/index.htm
Worldprofit Inc.	Edmonton	http://207.153.39.143/servicepage2.htm
Arizona		
Advanced Internet Solutions, Inc.	Scottsdale	http://www.advintsol.com/frontpage.htm
AWAK Internet Studio	Gilbert	http://www.awak.com/service.htm
Bluehawk Communications, Inc.	Glendale	http://fp.bluehawk.com/default.asp
CrystalTech	Peoria	http://www.crystaltech.com/frontpage.htm
FiestaNet Communications	Phoenix	http://www.fiestanet.com/fiesta/frontpagelink.htm
Internet Now, Inc	Tempe	http://fp.doitnow.com
Interwrx	Mesa	http://www.interwrx.com/iwrxfpsvcpage.htm
Systems Technology Group, Inc.	Phoenix	http://www.stglink.com/services/internet/hosting/default.asp
Virtualwebz.net	Tuscon	http://virtualwebz.net/fp2ksupported.htm
Arkansas		
Internet Partners of America	Fort Smith	http://home.ipa.net/services/svcpage1.htm
British Columbia		
Blaze Telecommunications Inc.	New Westminster	http://www.blaze.ca/frontpage.php
Corporate Web Solutions	Vancouver	http://www.cwshost.com/frontpage.htm
Datacom Consulting	Prince Rupert	http://www.inovadev.com/service.htm
MediaWeb Solutions	Kamloops	http://www.mwsolutions.com/hosting_f.html
NTonline Solutions Network	Chilliwack	http://www.ntonline.com/fp200.html
Pacific Online	Vancouver	http://www.paconline.net/solutions/frontpage.asp
Prematic Digital Systems Corp.	Saanichton	http://www.prematic.com/frontpage/fp.htm
Superb Internet	Vancouver	http://services.superb.net/fp.shtml

ISP Name	Location	URL
The Forest Industry Network	Nanaimo	http://www.forestindustry.com/fphosting/index.html
Webscape Internet Management Ltd.	Vancouver	http://www.web-scape.com/frontpage

California

007WebHosting.com FrontPage	LA	http://007WebHosting.com/
24biz.com	Garden Grove	http://www.24biz.com/frontpage.html
4thebest.net at Fowler Internet	Oakdale	http://www.4thebest.net/frontpage.htm
724 Hosting	Lompoch	http://www.724hosting.com/frontpage.htm
Advanced Technology Applications Inc	Lomita	http://www.advta.com/frontpage2000
Advantage Network	Santee	http://www.mswin.net/web_hosting.htm
American Business Web	Burbank	http://usbusinessweb.net/svcpage.htm
AtFreeWeb.com	Oxnard	http://www.atfreeweb.com/Support/svcpage.htm
Atlantis International	Santa Ana	http://www.atlantis-intl.com/frontpage/
AWWWsome Net Services	Redding	http://www.awwwsome.com/support/fp.htm
BigBiz Internet Services	Santa Clara	http://www.bigbiz.com/bigbiz/frontpage.phtml
CanZ LLC	Santa Monica	http://www.canz.com/fpage/default.htm
Catapult Information Solutions	Woodland Hills	http://www.catapult-is.com/frontpage2000.html
ComCity Corporation	Dublin	http://www.comcity.com/FrontPage2000/cfront.htm
Commercial Illusions	San Diego	http://www.commercial-illusions.com/Services/hosting/frontpage
Concentric Network Corporation	San Jose	http://www.concentric.net/web_solutions/host_frontpage.html
EarthLink Network Inc.	Pasadena	http://www.earthlink.net/business/hosting/webrelease.html
edition.net	Seal Beach	http://frontpage2000.edition.net
Edson Internet	La Habra	http://www.edson.net/fp2000.htm
Esosoft Corporation	Upland	http://www.esosoft.net/frontpage
Executive Web Services / YourHost.com	Huntington Beach	http://www.yourhost.com//index.html
Gottschalk Internet	Stockton	http://www.gotnet.net/fpservice.htm
Hexagon Net	Bakersfield	http://www.hexagon.net/FP2000/svcpage.htm
HostPro	Los Angeles	http://www.hostpro.net/solutions/frontpage/
Island Breeze Network Solutions	Corona	http://www.islandbreeze.com/svcpage.htm
IT Software Design Co.	Covina	http://www.itsoftware.com/frontpage.asp

| ITL America Inc | Marina del Rey | http://itl5.itlnet.com/frontpage.htm |

ISP Name	Location	URL
Jayscott Online	Alameda	http://www.jayscott.com/about/frontpage.asp
JKPWARE Systems Integration	Daly City	http://www.jkpware.com/services/hosting/svcpage.htm
Lightspeed Net	Bakersfield	http://frontpage.lightspeed.net
Millenia Internet Services, Inc	Signal Hill	http://www.millenia.com/hosting/FrontPage.htm
Mirada Information Services	La Mirada	http://www.LaMiradaBusiness.com/frontpage.htm
Netwood Communications	Los Angeles	http://www.netwood.net/frontpage.html
Nicheware, Inc.	Roseville	http://www.nichewareinc.com/svcpage.htm
PhoenixData	Brea	http://www.phoenixdata.com/frontpage.htm
Point & Click Consulting	Chatsworth	http://www.hosting4less.com/frontpage.html
Prime Internet Network	Tustin	http://www.primenetwork.net/sales/webhost.htm
RaapNet Inc.	Huntington Beach	http://www.raap.net/services/frontpag.htm
RealWebSite	Palo Alto	http://frontpage.realwebsite.com/
San Jose Web	San Jose	http://www.sanjoseweb.com/svcpage.htm
SCR Online	Vallejo	http://www.scronline.com/services/frontpageservice.htm
Simple Network Communications, Inc.	San Diego	http://www.simplenet.com/services/frontpage.html
SiteHosting.net	City of Industry	http://www.sitehosting.net/svcpage.htm
Snap Internet	Rancho Palos Verdes	http://www.snapinternet.com FrontPage2000/svcpage2000.htm
SPIV Technologies Group	San Jose	http://www.voicegateway.com/wpp/svcpage.htm
STATION 1	Santa Monica	http://www.station1.com/fphost.htm
Suite500 Web Hosting	Costa Mesa	http://www.suite500.net/FP2000.htm
The Haaverson Corporation	Livermore	http://www.haav.net/frontpage.htm
Three-D Technologies	Oxnard	http://www.three-d.net/svcpage.htm
TierraNet Inc.	San Diego	http://www.tierranet.com/frontpage2000.shtml
TRION Systems	San Luis Obispo	http://www.trion-systems.com/frontpage.asp
TST On Ramp, Inc.	Pomona	http://business.tstonramp.com/fp2000.htm
Ulink Internet	Carmichael	http://www.ulink.net/fp.htm
US InterSpace	San Francisco	http://www.us-interspace.com/svcpage.html
Virtual Sites	San Francisco	http://demont.v-site.net/svcframes.htm

Visual Trends, Inc.	Simi Valley	http://visualtrends.com/webhosting/fp2000.html

ISP Name	Location	URL
Colorado		
4DVISION LLC	Englewood	http://www.4dv.net/frontpage.htm
Advanced Instruments Corp	Littleton	http://www.ai.com/frontpage.htm
Colorado Online	Glen Haven	http://colorado.on-line.com/FrontPage/
Cottonwood Enterprises	Longmont	http://www.cwe.com/fp2000-prices.htm
E Street Communications	Denver	http://webhosting.estreet.com/frontpage/
GETYOUR.COM, Inc.	Colorado Springs	http://www.getyour.com/FrontPage.htm
Lorimer Network Research	Arvada	http://www.lornet.com/svcpage.htm
TMBS Connections	Thornton	http://www.tmbsbbs.com/tmbsfp.htm
Verio, Inc.	Englewood	http://www.verio.com/hosting/frontpage/
Web Panache	Denver	http://www.webpanache.com/hosting/fp2000.htm
Connecticut		
A Little Technology Shoppe, LLC	East Lyme	http://www.alts.net/fpinfo.html
Computer Peripherals Plus	Manchester	http://www.cpplus.com/frontpage/default.htm
CyberShore, Inc.	Madison	http://www.cshore.com/fp-welcome
InterTrek Technologies, LLC	Wallingford	http://www.intertrek.net/frontpage.htm
LexiConn Internet Services, Inc.	Colchester	http://www.lexiconn.com/frontpage2000.html
Delaware		
DelaNET / Logic Link, Inc.	New Castle	http://frontpage.delanet.com
Florida		
A Family-Net	Sarasota	http://frontpage2000.family-net.org
Acceleration	Gainesville	http://www.acceleration.net/frontpage/
Action Computers	Longwood	http://actsbbs.net/svcpage.htm
American Internet Technologies, Corp.	Delray Beach	http://www.americaninter.net/frontpage/
Applied Innovations	West Palm Beach	http://www.appliedi.net/frontpage/
Creative Data Concepts Limited, Inc.	Gulf Breeze	http://www.creativedata.net/msfrontpage2000.htm
Creative Pages	Venice	http://www.creative-pages.com/hosting.htm

Crystal Clear Concepts, Inc.	Tampa	http://www.CrystalClear.Net/Wpp.htm
DAYO Inc.	Deltona	http://www.dayo.net/svcpage.htm
DeZines Web Hosting	Boca Raton	http://www.Web-Hosting.com/nt/

ISP Name	Location	URL
dotSTAR	Pensacola	http://home.dotstar.net/fp.htm
E-mail on the Spot Inc.	Miami	http://www.eots.com/rates.htm
First Coast Online	Jacksonville	http://www.fcol.com/svcpage.htm
FutureSights, Inc.	St. Petersburg	http://www.futuresights.com/webhosting/comparison.ihtml?show=frontpage
FYINOW	Sunrise	http://www.fyinow.com/Moreinfo.htm
Gate1 Web Services	Fort Lauderdale	http://www.gate1.net/svcpage.htm
Hiway Technologies	Boca Raton	http://www.hiway.com/hosting/frontpage/
Host Depot, Inc.	Coral Springs	http://www.hostdepot.com/FrontPage.asp
iNNERHOST	Miami	http://www.innerhost.com/frontpage.asp
Internet Global Development Corp., Inc.	Coral Springs	http://www.igdc.com/svcpage.html
Internet Marketing 1, Inc	Fort Myers	http://im1.com/services/frontpage/index.htm
Internetco	Miami	http://www.internetco.net/web_hosting.html
JBM Computer Services, Inc.	Orlando	http://www.web-cycat.com/webhosting.htm
Kaiadoggi Designs	St. Petersburg	http://www.kdworld.com/wpp.htm
LiveWire Communications, Inc.	Gainesville	http://www.lwssl.net/frontpage/svcpage.htm
Netdor Internet	Fort Lauderdale	http://www.getsite.net/mssvc.htm
Netwide Access Technologies	Orlando	http://www.netwide.net/FrontPage2000.htm
Plugit.com	Pensacola	http://plugit.com/frontpage
PremierSite	Miami	http://www.premiersite.com/html/support/services/frontpage2000.htm
Rapid Systems FP2000.htm	Tampa	http://www.rapidsys.com/
Realacom	Ormond Beach	http://www.realacom.com/frontpage.htm
SYMO Technologies, Inc	Gainesville	http://www.symo.com/fp.html
ValueWeb	Deerfield Beach	http://www.valueweb.net/support/frontpage.html
WebStore Inc.	Miami Beach	http://fp2000.webstoreinc.com

Georgia

Atl-Connect	Atlanta	http://www.atlcon.net/frontpage2000.htm
Cybertron, Inc.	Atlanta	http://www.cybertronic.net/svcpage.htm
Hacom	Augusta	http://www.hacom.net/frontpag2.htm

IMC Online	Atlanta	http://imconline.net/imc/frontpage/frontpage1.htm
Interland Inc.	Atlanta	http://www.interland.net/wpp.htm
MindSpring	Atlanta	http://business.mindspring.com/frontpage.html

ISP Name	**Location**	**URL**
Need a Dot Com?	Alpharetta	http://needa.com/FrontPage
Romanweb	Rome	http://www.romanweb.com/frontpage2000
Sage Networks	Atlanta	http://www.sagenetworks.com/frontpage/
Savannah Wired	Savannah	http://hosting.savannahwired.com/frontpage.htm
WebWorks Southeast	Locust Grove	http://www.wwse.net/fp2000.htm

Hawaii

| Hawaii Internet Systems | Kaneohe | http://www.hi.net/support/frontpage.htm |

Idaho

First Step Internet	Moscow	http://www.fsr.net/services/frontpage.asp
Micron Internet Services	Boise	http://www.micron.net/prodserv/frontpg.html
USurf America, Inc	Boise	http://www.cyberhighway.net/frontpage/svcpage.htm

Illinois

AIS Network	Schaumburg	http://www.aisnetwork.net/hosting/frontpage2000.html
AlphaZone Solutions, LLC	Naperville	http://www.alphazone.com/fphosting.htm
Athens Hosting	Chicago	http://www.athenshost.com/fpAthens.asp
BCS Corporation	Skokie	http://www.bcschicago.com/services/hosting/
Business Consulting International	Schaumburg	http://www.bciltd.net/WebHost/svcpage.asp
CIFNet, Inc	Chicago	http://www.cifnet.com/services/fp.html
digital Chicago	Chicago	http://www.digitalchicago.net/services/hosting.htm
Fox Valley Internet, Inc.	Elgin	http://www.foxvalley.net/www/FrontPage?n
Host Experts	Chicago	http://www.hostexperts.net/frontpage.htm
Hostess Web Hosting	Rockford	http://www.hostess.com/frontpage.html
Internet Technologies, Inc.	Mount Prospect	http://www.itihome.com/frontpage.htm
JJC-IET WebServices	Joliet	http://www.jjciet.org/webservices/frontpage.htm

MTCO Communications	Metamora	http://www.mtco.com/internet/rates/frontpage.php3
NETISP, Inc.	Chicago	http://www.netisp.com/frontpage.html
People Technology	Hawthorn Woods	http://ptech.dynip.com/wpp/index.htm

ISP Name	Location	URL
Stargate Communications, Inc.	Oak Brook	http://www.stargate-network.com/frontpage.htm
Trout Spring	Chicago	http://www.troutspring.com/microsoft_frontpage_support.htm
XLSTAR Corporation	Champaign	http://www.xlstar.com/fpservice.htm

Indiana

A-Home-For-Your-Site	Muncie	http://www.a-home-for-your-site.com/frontpage/
BCi Internet Services	Highland	http://frontpage.internetbci.com
Corpis.com Inc.	Fort Wayne	http://www.corpis.com/frontpage
Corpsite	Fort Wayne	http://www.corpsite.com/pages/frontpage.html
Ohio Valley Wireless	Evansville	http://www.ovcwireless.net/svcpage.htm
On-Ramp Indiana	Carmel	http://www.ori.net/fp2000.htm
Rapidway, Inc.	Hobart	http://www.rapidway.com/frames/frontpage.htm
WHEK-Web, Inc.	Kendallville	http://www.whekweb.com/svcpage.htm

Iowa

ACES, Inc.	Waterloo	http://www.acesiowa.com/svcpage.htm
Hostin.com	Urbandale	http://www.hostin.com/services.htm

Kansas

Pen Publishing Interactive	Wichita	http://www.penpublishing.com/frontpage.htm

Kentucky

Chapel Services Inc	Richmond	http://www.chapel1.com/frontpage
Progress Printing Company Inc.	Owensboro	http://www.goprogress.net/frontpage_service.htm

Louisiana

InterVelocity, Inc.	Alexandria	http://www.intervelocity.com/fp2000.htm
Main Street Internet Service	New Iberia	http://www.msis.net/fp2000
Southeastern Internet Service Providers	Marrero	http://www.sispweb.com/FrontPage2000.htm

Maryland

AIM Corporation	Gaithersburg	http://www.aimcorporation.com/fp2k.htm
BitShop	College Park	http://www.bitshop.com/webhosting/whyfp.htm
CyberTec Computer Services	Reisterstown	http://www.takingcareofbusiness.com/frontpage

ISP Name	Location	URL
Internet Connection	Easton	http://internetconnection.net/frontpage.html
James S. Kay, Consulting	Laurel	http://www.jskay-consulting.com/hosting.htm

Massachusetts

Acunet.net	Marlboro	http://www.acunet.net/fp2ksrvcpg/svcpage.htm
Advanced Commerce Solutions, Inc.	Saugus	http://www.acomsolutions.com/hosting.
Ballou Internet Services, Inc.	Tyngsboro	http://www.ballou.net/frontpage/
CoServers Express, Inc.	Ipswich	http://www.coservers.com/hosting/fplisting.htm
DataPro Services, Inc.	Ashby	http://hosting.dpsinc.com
GlobalDrum Internet	Hopkinton	http://www.globaldrum.net/data/frontpage.html
Strauss Software Services, LLC	Wrentham	http://www.strausoft.com/msfp/fp2000.htm
Technology Horizons	Amherst	http://www.th.net/th_fpage.html
Tripod, Inc.	Williamstown	http://www.tripod.com/build/frontpage/

Michigan

Adaptive.net	Troy	http://www.adaptive.net/hosting-fp.html
Avalon Systems, Inc.	Flint	http://www.customweb.net/wpp
Baraga Telephone Company	Baraga	http://info.up.net/hosting/frontpage.html
BECamation	Edwardsburg	http://www.becamation.com/wpp.htm
Biznet Internet Solutions	Southfield	http://frontpage.getbiz.net
CQL Incorporated	Grand Rapids	http://www.cqlcorp.com/FrontPageServices.htm
Cyberstep Electronic Marketing	Rochester	http://www.cyberstep.net/hosting/
dotCOM Productions, Inc.	Holland	http://www.dotcomproductions.com/frontpage2000.stm
Inetsolution, Inc.	Almont	http://www.inetsolution.com/frontpage.html
Iserv Company, Inc.	Grand Rapids	http://frontpage.iserv.net/
Molarnet Technologies, Inc.	Saginaw	http://www.molar.net/frontpage.htm
Webproze Dotcom Inc	Kalamazoo	http://www.webproze.com/fpservice.htm

Minnesota

Acme Internet	Minneapolis	http://www.acmeinternet.com/frontpage/

HostForce	St. Paul	http://www.hostforce.com/frontpage
Outlook Technologies, Inc.	St. Paul	http://www.outtech.com/hosting.htm

Missouri

1st Choice International	Maryland Heights	http://www.1stChoiceSite.com/frontpage.htm

ISP Name	Location	URL
CommuniTech.Net Inc.	St. Joseph	http://www.communitech.net/frontpage
Dependable Internet, L.L.C.	Springfield	http://www.dpnd.net/fpentry.htm
E-Builders, LLC	Elsberry	http://e-builders.com/fp/svcpage.htm
HTTP Solutions	Ballwin	http://www.httpsolutions.net/frontpage.asp
JCN Internet Services	Festus	http://web.jcn.net/fphosting.htm
KCnet, Inc.	North Kansas City	http://www.kcnet.com/html/fphosting.html
Mr. Woofus Hosting	Dittmer	http://www.mrwoofus.com/svcpage.htm
The Miller Group	St. Louis	http://www.themillergroup.com/internet/fphosting.htm
United States Internet Presence Provider	Springfield	http://www.usipp.com/FrontPage2000.htm

Nebraska

Jasniam, LLC	Omaha	http://www.hostmydomain.com/fp2000.shtml

Nevada

Action Web	Henderson	http://www.actionweb.com/hosting/frontpage.phtml
MagicImage Corp	Reno	http://www.magicimage.net/FPSupport.htm
Net-Tek	Las Vegas	http://www.net-tek.net/svcpage.htm
virtualhosting.com	Henderson	http://virtualhosting.com/frontpage

New Hampshire

eNET Value, Inc.	Amherst	http://www.enetvalue.com/fp2000page.htm
Web Serve Pro	Hudson	http://www.webservepro.com/wpp

New Jersey

Argos Networks	Maywood	http://www.ArgosWeb.net/Services/FPHosting.shtm
Asch WebHosting Inc.	Toms River	http://www.aschwebhosting.com/fp2kservice.htm
AT&T Web Site Services	Lincroft	http://www.ipservices.att.com/wss/index.html
Celerity Communications LLC	West Caldwell	http://www.celeritycomm.com/internet/frontpage2000.htm
CMB Systems Net	Dayton	http://www.cmbsystems.net/

		frontpage/
FSIWebs	Glen Rock	http://www.fsiwebs.com/Design99/FP2000/servicepage.htm
Gilford Graphics International	Toms River	http://www.gilfordgraphics.com/frontpage/index.html
HiSpeed Hosting	Hoboken	http://www.hispeedhosting.com/frontpagehosting.htm

ISP Name	Location	URL
Internet Images Worldwide, Inc.	Hoboken	http://www2.inet-images.com/svcpage.html
Skywaves/NewSource Global Web Commerce	Wyckoff	http://fp2000.skywaves.net
US InfiNet, Inc.	Union City	http://www.usinfinet.com/web_host/fpage.asp
VF Technologies, LLC	Hoboken	http://www.vftech.com/services/frontpage.htm
Web Publishing and Development Corp.	Bloomsbury	http://www.wpdcorp.com/MSFP2000.htm
Webb Solutions, Inc.	Fair Lawn	http://www.webb-solutions.com/svcpage.htm

New Mexico

Arriba Computer Solutions Hosting	Albuquerque	http://www.arriba.net/hosting
Auburn SeeWolf	Tijeras	http://www.sbaccess.net/frontpage.htm

New York

AWI.tech	Brooklyn	http://www.awitech.com/FrontPage2000/default.htm
BlueSpring.com, Inc.	New York	http://www.bluespring.com/services/hosting/frontpage.htm
CBS Co./ WebRamp	Albany	http://www.webramp.net/webramp2/services2.htm
Cornells Internet Services	Eastchester	http://www.eastchester.net/frontpg.htm
DELTA internet services, Inc.	Farmingdale	http://www.hostasite.com/services/frontpage.html
Digitware, LLC	Flushing	http://www.webmage.com/frontpage/frontpage2000.asp
Get On The Web Internet Services	Niskayuna	http://www.ntwebhosting.com/frontpage/
Gotham Web Services	New York	http://www.gothamweb.com/fp2000/
Interactive Internet Corporation	Westbury	http://www.interactive-internet.com/frontpage.htm
MerlinWeb	Brooklyn	http://www.merlinweb.net/services/fp2k.htm
Micro Training Center	Olean	http://wpp.microtraining.com
Network Technology Services, Inc.	Brooklyn	http://www.nets.net/frontpage.htm
New York Web Works	Rochester	http://nywebworks.com/fp2000.html
OnePine Internet	New York	http://www.onepine.com/frontpage2000.htm

PoweredBy.com	Rochester	http://www.PoweredBy.com/frontpage.htm
Stafford Associates	Setauket	http://www.staffordnet.com/frontpage.htm
Synapse Imaging	Ronkonkoma	http://synapseimaging.com/frontpage2000.html
TELEcomputers Services	Freeport	http://www.telesites.net/frontpage/index.html

ISP Name	Location	URL
Total Hosting	West Islip	http://www.totalhosting.com/fp/svcpage.htm
TTSG	New York	http://www.ttsg.com/frontpage/fp2000.php3
ValueWebHosting.com Inc.	Williamsville	http://valuewebhosting.com/rcenter/resources/frontpage/frontpage.htm
Vision Interactive Systems	Apalachin	http://www.visionis.com/hosting/frontpage.htm
Web Genius	Bellerose	http://www.web-genius.com/frontpage2000.asp

North Carolina

ACTplus.net	Fuquay-Varina	http://www.actplus.net/frontpage.htm
American Data Technology, Inc.	Durham	http://www.localweb.com/frontpage/
CyberSharks.net	Winterville	http://www.cybersharks.net/frontpage2000.htm
eXodite Dimensions	Fayetteville	http://www.exodite.net/webservices/fp2000svcpage.asp
Pinnacle View Web Hosting sources/	Pinnacle	http://www.pvwh.com/home/re-add-ons/frontpage/default.htm
WEBDEV+	Cornelius	http://www.webdevplus.com/hosting.htm

Nova Scotia

Coastal Watch Information Services Ltd.	Dartmouth	http://www.coastalwatch.net/frontpage2000

Ohio

Bodi & Associates, Inc.	Lakewood	http://www.clevenet.com/FrontPage-hosting.htm
Computer Resources	Port Clinton	http://corporate-hosting.net/frontpage.htm
DACOR Internet Services	Bowling Green	http://www.dacor.net/fpsvcpage.htm
GCIS, Inc.	Cincinnati	http://surpass.gcis.net/frontp
GO Concepts, Inc.	Lebanon	http://www.go-concepts.com/frontpage.htm
HCST*Net	Beavercreek	http://www.hcst.net/fpsvcpage.htm
HMC Ltd, Inc.	Bellevue	http://www.hmcltd.net/fp2000/index.html

ISP Name	Location	URL
Holland Computers Internet Services	Elyria	http://www.hollandcomputers.com/webhosting/Pricing.htm
Infovue.net	Medina	http://www.infovue.net/fp_services.htm
M&A Computer Services	New Lebanon	http://www.tristateweb.com/frontpage.html
Mango Bay Internet	Cleveland	http://www.mango-bay.com
Millennium Web, Ltd.	Brecksville	http://www.mwhost.com/whp.htm

ISP Name	Location	URL
NetLink Services, Inc.	Macedonia	http://www.getinfo.net/frontpag.htm
SelfNet, Inc.	Dublin	http://www.selfnet.com/FP2000
SRC Systems, Inc.	Cincinnati	http://www.srcsystems.com/frontpage
Wspin.com	Dayton	http://www.wspin.com/serviceweb/svcpage.htm

Oklahoma

biz2web Internet Services	Oklahoma City	http://www.biz2web.com/rates
Internet-Duncan, Inc.	Duncan	http://www.texhoma.net/frontpage.htm

Ontario

Alex Technologies Inc.	Toronto	http://www.alextec.com/frontpage.htm
Elehost Web Design Inc.	Toronto	http://www.elehost.com/Services/Frontpage/frontpage.html
Interhop Network Services Inc.	Toronto	http://www.interhop.com/services/hosting/fphosting.html
I-Wiz	Nepan	http://www.i-wiz.com/frontpage.htm
Justweb Inc.	London	http://hosting.justweb.net/frontpage/
LOG ON Internet Solutions	Chatsworth	http://log.on.ca/frontpage
MicroAge Computer Centres	Thunder Bay	http://www.microage-tb.com/servicepage.htm
MultiHome Web Hosting Service	Sarnia	http://www.multihome.com/fp.html
Nexus Data Systems	Brampton	http://www.nexusds.com/frontpage2000/
SoftCom Technology Consulting Inc.	Toronto	http://www.softcomca.com/fp2000.html
Vastcom Network Inc.	Markham	http://www.vastcom.net/frontpage/FP2000.htm

Oregon

AWEBHOST	Portland	http://awebhost.com/frontpage.htm
Cutting Edge Webs	Terrebonne	http://www.ceeserve.com/svcpage.htm
Global Frontiers, Inc.	Milwaukie	http://www.globalfrontiers.com/services/frontpage.html
Internet Business Services, Inc.	Medford	http://www.ibsnet.net/frontp.htm
Rendezvous Business Connections (RBC)	Portland	http://www.renpdx.com/frontpage.htm

Pennsylvania

ISP Name	Location	URL
AmeriHost International	Broomall	http://www.amerihost.net/frontpage.htm
BlackBoard Networks	Bristol	http://websrv.bboard.com/svcpage.htm
BrandywineNet	Oxford	http://www.brandywine.net/frontpage.htm
Dynamic Net, Inc.	Womelsdorf	http://www.dynamicnet.net/services/fpwebhosting.htm

ISP Name	Location	URL
ePodWorks.net	Willow Grove	http://www.epodworks.net/link/ms/frontpage.htm
InfoQuest	Harrisburg	http://www.fptoday.com/rates/compare.htm
Netconex, Inc.	Lancaster	http://www.netconexinc.com/frontpage.htm
NetReach, Inc.	Fort Washington	http://home.netreach.net/frontpage/
ParknBuild.com	Philadelphia	http://www.ParknBuild.com/frontpage/
Pittsburgh FamilyNet	Pittsburgh	http://www.pghfamily.net/member/fp2000/svcpage.htm
Sawyer & Associates Marketing	Wellsboro	http://www.youu-net.com/fphost.htm
SiteHost International	Broomall	http://www.sitehost.net/microsoft/svcpage.htm
Synergration, Inc.	Wayne	http://www.synergration.com/Internet/iWPP.htm
Web Space Outlet	State College	http://www.wso.net/frontpage.htm

Quebec

ISP Name	Location	URL
Ronnex inc.	Montreal	http://www.startius.com/web/english.html
Télénet Informatique Inc.	Chicoutimi	http://www.telenetinfo.com/frontpageen.htm

Rhode Island

ISP Name	Location	URL
Internet Listing Service/401business.com	Warwick	http://401business.com/frontpage2000/
MontegoNet Solutions	Middletown	http://www.montegonet.com/fp2000.htm
Power Computer Systems, Inc.	Providence	http://www.powercomputers.com/fpservice.htm

Saskatchewan

ISP Name	Location	URL
Allstar Technologies Canada	Regina	http://internet.allstartech.com/frontpg.htm

South Carolina

ISP Name	Location	URL
Burkett Network Carolina, LLC	West Columbia	http://www.networkcarolina.com/main.asp?pageID=4
CETlink	Rock Hill	http://www.cetlink.net/

| | | frontpage.html |
| Genesis Consulting | Ladson | http://www.genesis-consulting.com/ hosting.asp |

Tennessee

| VTservers | Memphis | http://vtserve.com/frontpage.htm |

ISP Name	Location	URL
Texas		
@247IP.com	Dallas	http://247ip.com/FrontPage/
@dfwwebs.com	Dallas	http://@dfwwebs.com/info-frontpage.htm
1goodsite.com	Houston	http://www.1goodsite.com/frontpage.htm
2coolWEB	Dallas	http://www.2coolweb.com/fp2000.htm
ABC Hosting	Richardson	http://www.abcHosting.net/frontpage.htm
Amplified Imaging, Inc.	San Antonio	http://www.amplifiedimaging.com/Web_Page_Hosting/svcpage.htm
Cartama Consulting LLC	San Antonio	http://www.cartama.net/frontpage.htm
CI Host, Inc.	Bedford	http://www.cihost.com/frontpage.html
CommerceStreet.com	Arlington	http://www.commercestreet.com/HostingFrontPage2000.htm
Hawk Internet Services	Fort Worth	http://www.hawkpci.net/services/hosting/frontpage.htm
Hill Country Web	Spicewood	http://hillcountryweb.com/frontpage
Iland Internet Solution Corporation	Houston	http://www.iland.com/frontpage.html
OptiQuest Internet Services	Spring	http://frontpage.optiquest.net
PDQ.Net, Inc.	Houston	http://www.pdq.net/services/fp2k.htm
QuantumHost	Rockwall	http://quantumhost.net/frontpage2000/
Right Step Technologies	Hurst	http://www.right-step.com/frontpage2000.asp
SmartByte Inc.	Dallas	http://www.smartbyte.net/fp
Webspinner Hosting & Design Solutions	Garland	http://www.webspinner.net/fp2000.htm
WebWax	Carrollton	http://www.webwax.net/FrontPage2000/
Worldwide Systems Analysis	Humble	http://www.wsawebs.com/fp2000.htm

Utah

| Computer Solutions | Salt Lake City | http://www.csolutions.net/frontpage.html |
| Internet Servers Incorporated | Orem | http://www.iserver.com/support/addonhelp/frontpage2000/index.html |

| LightSpeed Internet Services, LLC | Provo | http://lightspeedweb.com/frontpage/ |

Vermont

| Burlee Networks | Burlington | http://www.burlee.com/svcpage.htm |

Virginia

| Access Technology, Inc. | Richmond | http://www.accesstechnology.net/frontpage |

ISP Name	Location	URL
ACS Web Services Group	Gainesville	http://web.advcs.com/hosting_frontpage.h
Bell Atlantic	Falls Church	http://www.baweb.com/msfp/
DcMetroNet.com	Fairfax	http://www.yibm.com/rates.htm
Digital Expressions, Inc.	Virginia Beach	http://www.digiexpress.com/fp2000.htm
GCR Company	South Boston	http://www.gcronline.com/fpweb
Internet & Information Solutions, Inc	Arlington	http://www.TrueServer.com/frontpage.htm
Lanexa International, LLC	Lanexa	http://www.lanexa.net/fp2000.htm
Micro Concepts of Chesterfield	Midlothian	http://www.mcws.net/frontpage.html
PSINet	Herndon	http://www.psinet.com/hosting/frontpage/
TechnoSphere Consulting, inc.	Fairfax	http://www.technosc.com/WPPService2000.htm
World Data Network, Inc.	Reston	http://www.wdn.com/fpagewdn.html

Washington

AAces.com	Blaine	http://aaces.com/wpp
Cyber World Internet Services	Spokane	http://www.thesitehost.com/fp2000.htm
FireTrail Internet Services, Inc	Everett	http://www.firetrail.com/FrontPage
GeckoTech, Inc.	Bellevue	http://www.GeckoTech.com/home/FrontPage.asp
Ironwood Express Web Services	Seattle	http://www.iewebs.net/msfront.htm
Jmp Interact Web Services	Tacoma	http://www.citywalks.com/jmp/frontpage.htm
Kalliopi International	Seattle	http://www.kalliopi.com/prodWHST.htm
Rapidsystem	Spokane	http://www.rapidsystem.net/frontpage.htm
VServers	Kirkland	http://www.vservers.com/features/fp2000.html
Webstoresnw.net	Burien	http://www.webstoresnw.net/frontpage.htm

Wisconsin

Alexssa Enterprises, Ltd.	West Bend	http://www.alexssa.net/Services/svcpage.htm
Comstar Technologies	Waukesha	http://www.wauknet.com/frontpage.html
The Jungling Company, Inc	West Allis	http://www.jnet.net/Microsoftdefault.htm

Quick Reference

Lesson 1: Planning a Web Site

To import a Web

1 On the File menu, point to New, and click Web.
2 Click the Import Web Wizard icon.
3 Specify the location of the new Web.
4 Click the From A Source Directory Of Files option, and select the Include Subfolders check box.
5 Click the Browse button, browse to the Web folder, and then click OK.
6 Click Next twice, and click Finish.

To change views

● Click the Page icon to view the currently selected Web page.
● Click the Normal tab to edit a Web page.
● Click the HTML tab to view the HTML code.
● Click the Preview tab to preview a Web page.
● Click the Folders icon to view folders and files.
● Click the Reports icon to view the current Web report.
● Click the Navigation icon to view the navigation tree diagram.
● Click the Hyperlinks icon to view the hyperlinks diagram.
● Click the Tasks icon to view the Web task list.

To close a Web page

● Click the Close button in the top-right corner of the Web page.

To close a Web

● On the File menu, click Close Web.

To open a Web

1 On the File menu, click Open Web.
2 Browse to the Web that you want to open.
3 Click the Open button.

To browse the Internet

1   Connect to the Internet, and double-click the Web browser icon on the Windows desktop.

2   In the Address bar, type the URL for the site that you want the browser to display, and press Enter.

Lesson 2: Creating a Web Site

To create a Web site using a wizard

1   On the File menu, point to New, and click Web.

2   In the New dialog box, click the wizard that you want to use.

3   In the Specify A Location Of The New Web box, type the location and name of the new Web.

4   Click OK, and click Next.

To create a Web using a template

1   On the File menu, point to New, and click Web.

2   In the New dialog box, click the template that you want to use.

3   In the Specify A Location Of The New Web box, type the location and name of the new Web.

4   Click OK.

To create a Web page in Page view

1   On the File menu, point to New, and click Page.

2   In the New dialog box, click the template that you want to use and click OK.

To title a Web page

1   On the Standard toolbar, click the Save button.

2   In the File Name box, type the new name, and click Save.

To add and format text

1   Make sure that the Web page is displayed in Page view.

2   Type the text that you want to add to the page (but do not press Enter).

3   Click the Style down arrow, and click a style to apply to the text.

4   Use the Formatting toolbar to apply any additional formatting.

To change Web page properties

1 In the Folder List, right-click the file that you want to rename, and click Properties on the shortcut menu.

2 In the Title box, type the new name for the page, and click the Summary tab.

3 Type the text that you want for the comment, and click OK.

4 On the Standard toolbar, click the Save button.

To preview a Web Page

● Click the Preview tab at the bottom of the FrontPage window.
Or

● On the Standard toolbar, click the Preview In Browser button.

To move and organize files in Folders view.

1 On the Views bar, click the Folders icon.

2 On the File menu, point to New, and click Folder.

3 Type a name for the folder, and press Enter.

4 Drag the files that you want to move into the new folder.

5 Double-click the folder to display its contents.

To move and organize files in Navigation view

1 On the Views bar, click the Navigation icon.

2 Drag the file that you want to move from the Folder List into Navigation view.

3 Drag any other pages that you want to link to the first page into Navigation view.

4 Continue to drag pages from the Folder List to Navigation view until all pages are organized.

5 On the Standard toolbar, click the Save button.

To view and print a Web's structure

1 On the Views bar, click the Navigation icon.

2 On the File menu, click Print.

3 Specify printing options, and click OK.

Lesson 3: Linking Web Pages

To link to a Web page in the current Web

1 Select the text that you want to make a hyperlink.

2 On the Insert menu, click Hyperlink, and browse to the target file.

3 Select the target file, and click OK.

To link to a Web page on the Internet

1   Select the text that you want to make a hyperlink.
2   On the Insert menu, click Hyperlink.
3   On the Standard toolbar, click the Preview In Browser button.
4   In the Web browser, connect to the site to which you want to create a hyperlink.
5   Press Alt+Tab to switch to FrontPage, and click OK.

To test hyperlinks

1   On the Standard toolbar, click the Preview In Browser button.
2   Click the hyperlink you want to test.

    Or

●   In Page view, hold down Ctrl, and click the hyperlink that you want to test.

To create a link to an e-mail address

1   Select the text that you want to make a hyperlink.
2   On the Insert menu, click Hyperlink, and then click the E-mail button.
3   Type the e-mail address you want to link to, and click OK twice.

To edit a hyperlink

1   Right-click the hyperlink that you want to edit, and click Hyperlink Properties.
2   In the Edit Hyperlink dialog box, browse to the new target file.
3   Click the new hyperlink target, and click OK.

To change hyperlink text

1   Select the hyperlink text that you want to change.
2   Type the new text.

To delete a hyperlink

1   Right-click the hyperlink text that you want to delete, and click Hyperlink Properties.
2   Press Delete, and click OK.

To create a bookmark on a Web page

1   Select the text that you want to make a bookmark.

    Or

    Place the insertion point where you want to make a bookmark.
2   On the Insert menu, click Bookmark, and click OK.

To create a hyperlink to a bookmark

1 Select the text you want to make a hyperlink.

2 On the Insert menu, click Hyperlink, browse to the target file, and then click the target file.

3 Click the Bookmark down arrow, click the desired bookmark, and then click OK.

To test a bookmark

1 On the Standard toolbar, click the Preview In Browser button.

2 Click the hyperlink that you want to test.

To delete a bookmark

1 Right-click the bookmark that you want to delete.

2 On the shortcut menu, click Bookmark Properties.

3 In the Other Bookmarks On This Page list, click the bookmark that you want to delete, and click the Clear button.

To create an image map

1 On the Web page, click where you want to insert the image.

2 On the Insert menu, point to Picture, and click From File.

3 Browse to the location of the image file, click the image file, and then click OK.

4 Click the image on the Web page.

5 On the Pictures toolbar, click the Rectangular Hotspot button, and draw a hotspot on the image.

6 In the Create Hyperlink dialog box, select the file that you want to create a hyperlink to, and click OK.

To test an image map

1 On the Standard toolbar, click the Preview In Browser button.

2 Move the mouse pointer over the image. When the mouse pointer turns from an arrow to a pointing hand, click the image.

3 On the toolbar of the Web browser, click the Back button.

4 Repeat steps 2 and 3 until you have tested all the hotspot hyperlinks.

Lesson 4: Adding Style to Web Pages

To apply a FrontPage theme to a Web

1 On the Format menu, click Theme.

2 In the Themes list, click the theme that you want to apply to the Web.

3 Select the desired options for the theme.

4 Click the All Pages option in the top-left corner of the dialog box, and click OK.

To modify a theme

1   On the Format menu, click Theme.

2   In the Themes dialog box, click the Modify button, and click the button for the theme characteristic that you want to modify.

3   Make the desired changes in the Modify Theme dialog box, and click OK twice.

4   Click Yes to save the modified theme.

To delete a theme

1   On the Format menu, click Theme.

2   In the Apply Theme To section of the dialog box, click the All Pages option.

3   In the Themes list, click No Theme, and click OK.

To add a marquee

1   Click the desired location for the marquee.

2   On the Insert menu, point to Component, and click Marquee.

3   In the Text box, type the text that you want the marquee to display and click OK.

To customize a marquee

1   Right-click the marquee that you want to modify.

2   In the Marquee Properties dialog box, change the properties that you want to modify, and click OK.

To format marquee text

1   Right-click the marquee, and click Font on the shortcut menu.

2   Adjust the marquee font and text size as needed, and click OK.

To add a hit counter to a Web page

1   Display the Web page in Page view, and click the desired location for the hit counter.

2   Type the desired caption, and press the Spacebar.

3   On the Insert menu, point to Component, and click Hit Counter.

4   Adjust the hit counter style and properties, and click OK.

To include one Web page inside another

1   Create the Web page that you want to include.

2   Display the Web page on which you want to include the new Web page, and click the desired location.

3   On the Insert menu, point to Component, and click Include Page.

4   Click the Browse button, browse to the Web page to be included, and click OK.

To create a header style sheet

1   In Page view, display the Web page for which you want to create a style sheet.

2   On the Format menu, click Style.

3   If necessary, click the List down arrow, and click All HTML Tags to display all Web page styles in the Styles list.

4   In the Styles list, click the style that you want to modify, and click the Modify button.

5   In the Modify Style dialog box, click the Format button, and click the desired style attribute in the Format list.

6   Make the desired changes, and click OK three times.

To use the Format Painter

1   Select the characters of paragraph that have the formatting that you want to copy.

2   On the Standard toolbar, click the Format Painter button, and select the text to which you want to apply the formatting.

Lesson 5: Formatting Web Pages

To create a bulleted list

1   Click the page location where you want to start the list.

2   On the Formatting toolbar, click the Bullets button, and type the list items, pressing Enter after each item.

To format bullets in a bulleted list

1   Right-click one of the bullets, and click List Properties on the shortcut menu.

2   Select a style.

3   Click OK.

To convert existing text to a bulleted list

1   Click the page location where you want to start the list.

2   On the Formatting toolbar, click the Bullets button.

3   Type the list items, pressing Enter after each item.

To create a numbered list

1   Click the page location where you want to start the list.

2   On the Formatting toolbar, click the Numbering button.

3   Type the list items, pressing Enter after each item.

To format numbers in a numbered list

1   Right-click one of the numbers.

2   Click List Properties on the shortcut menu, and select a style.

3   Click OK.

To change the starting number of a list

1   Right-click one of the bullets.

2   Click List Properties, and type the desired number in the Start At box.

3   Click OK.

To convert existing text to a numbered list

●   Select the text, and click the Numbering button on the Formatting toolbar.

To insert a table

1   Click the desired page location.

2   On the Table menu, point to Insert, click Table, and enter the number of rows and columns.

3   Click OK.

To insert text in a table cell

●   Click in the cell, and type the desired text.

To format text in one or more table cells

1   Select the text in the cell(s), and right-click the selected text.

2   Click Cell Properties, Font, or Paragraph, and make the changes.

3   Click OK.

To resize a table row or column

●   Drag a border of the row or column to the appropriate location.

To change the border of a table

1   Right-click a border.

2   Click Table Properties on the shortcut menu.

3   Make changes as desired in the Table Properties dialog box.

4   Click OK.

Lesson 6: Adding Multimedia to Web Pages

To insert a photo on a Web page

1   Click the desired location on the Web page.
2   On the Insert menu, point to Picture, and click From File.
3   Browse to the desired file, select it, and then click OK.

To search the Clip Art Gallery

1   On the Insert menu, point to Picture, and click Clip Art.
2   In the Search For Clips box, type a keyword for the picture, sound, or motion clip you want to search for, and press Enter.

To insert clip art on a Web page

1   Click the desired location on the Web page.
2   On the Insert menu, point to Picture, and click Clip Art.
3   Click the desired clip art, and click the Insert Clip icon on the pop-up menu.

To insert an image in a table cell

1   Click in the desired table cell.
2   On the Insert menu, point to Picture, and click From File.
3   Select the image to insert, and click OK twice.

    Or

1   Click in the desired table cell.
2   On the Insert menu, point to Picture, and click Clip Art.
3   Click the image to insert, and click the Insert Clip button.

To create an image thumbnail

●   Click the image on the Web page, and click the Auto Thumbnail button on the Pictures toolbar.

To move image files to the Images folder

1   On the Views bar, click the Folders icon.
2   Click the Type button in the top of the file list.
3   Select the files that you want to move, and drag them to the Images folder in the Folder List.

To resize an image

●   Click the image to select it, and drag one of its resize handles.

To specify alternative text for an image

1   Right-click the image, and on the shortcut menu, click Picture Properties.

2   Click in the Text box, type the alternative text, and then click OK.

To add text over an image

1   Click the image to which you want to add text, and click the Text button on the Pictures toolbar.

2   Click OK.

3   Use the handles at the edges of the text box to resize the text box.

4   Type the text that you want to add over the image.

5   Format the text as desired.

To add a background sound to a Web page

1   Right-click a blank area of the Web page, and on the shortcut menu, click Page Properties.

2   Click Browse, select the desired sound file, and then click OK twice.

To add a motion clip directly to a Web page

1   Click the desired location on the Web page.

2   On the Insert menu, point to Picture, and click Video.

3   Select the desired motion clip, and click OK.

To link to a motion clip

1   Select and right-click the text or image for the link.

2   On the shortcut menu, click Hyperlink.

3   Select the desired video file, and click OK.

Lesson 7: Publishing a Web

To check spelling on an entire Web

1   On the Views bar, click the Navigation icon.

2   On the Tools menu, click Spelling.

3   Verify that the Entire Web option is selected, and click Start.

4   In the Page list, double-click the page that you want to check.

5   Click Next Document to check another page.

To check spelling on a single Web page

1   In the Folder List, double-click the page that you want to check.

2   On the Tools menu, click Spelling.

3   When the spelling check is complete, click OK.

To change a file name in Folders view and update its hyperlinks

1   In the Folder List, right-click the file that you want to rename.
2   On the shortcut menu, click Rename.
3   Type the new name for the file, and press Enter.
4   Click Yes.

To publish a Web locally

1   On the File menu, click Publish Web.
2   In the Specify The Location To Publish Your Web box, type the folder name where you want to publish the Web.
3   Click Publish.

To rename a Web

1   On the Tools menu, click Web Settings.
2   In the Web Name box, delete the default text.
3   Type the new name, and click OK.

To update a Web on the server

1   If necessary, connect to the Internet or intranet.
2   On the File menu, click Publish Web.
3   Click Options, and select the desired update option.
4   In the Specify The Location To Publish Your Web To box, type the URL of the Web server and Web folder on the server.
5   Click Publish.
6   Type your user name and password, and click OK.

Lesson 8: Managing and Enhancing a Web

To use Reports view

1   On the Views bar, click the Reports icon.
2   In Reports view, double-click the line of the individual report that you want to display.

To change Reports view options

1   On the Tools menu, click Options.
2   Click the Reports View tab.
3   Make the desired changes.
4   Click OK.

To create and assign a task

1   On the Views bar, click the Tasks icon.

2   On the File menu, point to New, and click Task.

3   Click in the Task Name box, and type the task name.

4   Click in the Assigned To box, and type the person's name to whom you're assigning the task.

5   Click in the Description box, and type a description of the task.

6   Click OK.

To perform a task

1   On the Views bar, click Tasks.

2   Double-click the task that you want to perform, and click Start Task.

3   Make the desired changes.

4   On the Standard toolbar, click the Save button.

5   Click Yes to mark the task as completed.

Or

Right-click the task in the tasks list, and click Mark As Completed on the shortcut menu.

To view and sort tasks in Tasks view

1   On the Views bar, click the Tasks icon.

2   Click a column heading to sort the tasks by that column.

To create a table of contents

1   On the Views bar, click the Page icon, and click the New button on the Standard toolbar.

2   On the Insert menu, point to Component, and click Table Of Contents.

3   In the Table Of Contents Properties dialog box, make any desired changes, and click OK.

Or

On the File menu, point to New, and click Page. Click the Table Of Contents template icon, and click OK.

To animate text with dynamic HTML

1   On the Views bar, click the Page icon.

2   Select the text that you want to animate.

3   On the Format menu, click Dynamic HTML Effects to display the DHTML Effects toolbar.

4   On the DHTML Effects toolbar, select the event to trigger the effect, the type of effect, and the settings for the effect.

5   Click the Close button on the DHMTL Effects toolbar, and save the Web page.

To create special transition effects

1   On the Format menu, click Page Transition.

2   Select the event to trigger the effect, and specify the number of seconds for the effect to last.

3   Select the desired effect, and click OK.

To create a search page

1   On the Views bar, click the Page icon.

2   On the File menu, point to New, and click Page.

3   In the New dialog box, click the Search Page icon.

4   Click OK, and modify the search page as needed.

Index

Italicized page numbers
indicate figures and illustrations.

ActiveEducation and Microsoft Press

Microsoft FrontPage 2000 Step by Step Courseware has been created by the professional trainers and writers at ActiveEducation, Inc., to the exacting standards you've come to expect from Microsoft Press. Together, we are pleased to present this training guide.

ActiveEducation creates top-quality information technology training content that teaches essential computer skills for today's workplace. ActiveEducation courses are designed to provide the most effective training available and to help people become more productive computer users. Each ActiveEducation course, including this book, undergoes rigorous quality control, instructional design, and technical review procedures to ensure that the course is instructionally and technically superior in content and approach.

ActiveEducation (*www.activeeducation.com*) courses are available in book form and on the Internet.

Microsoft Press is the book publishing division of Microsoft Corporation, the leading publisher of information about Microsoft products and services. Microsoft Press is dedicated to providing the highest quality computer books and multimedia training and reference tools that make using Microsoft software easier, more enjoyable, and more productive.

About the Authors

Scott Palmer has worked in the computer industry for 18 years—almost since its inception. As a programmer, author, and teacher, he has written about computer technology for *The Wall Street Journal, USA Today, Info World, PC World, PC Techniques, Government Computer News,* and many other publications. A former distinguished teacher at Indiana University, he has been teaching people to use computers since 1981. Currently, he conducts computer training, programs, and consults. He is the author of 16 computer books.

Ron Pronk is the author of more than a dozen books on computers, including *Windows 3.1 Insider* (John Wiley & Sons) and *Digital Camera Companion* (Coriolis Group Books). He is a two-time recipient of the Award of Excellence from the Society for Technical Communicators and has served as an instructional design consultant for such companies as Delmar Publishing, Mitchell Press, South-Western Publishing, West Publishing, Coriolis Group Books, and National Computer Systems.

MICROSOFT LICENSE AGREEMENT
Book Companion CD

IMPORTANT—READ CAREFULLY: This Microsoft End-User License Agreement ("EULA") is a legal agreement between you (either an individual or an entity) and Microsoft Corporation for the Microsoft product identified above, which includes computer software and may include associated media, printed materials, and "online" or electronic documentation ("SOFTWARE PRODUCT"). Any component included within the SOFTWARE PRODUCT that is accompanied by a separate End-User License Agreement shall be governed by such agreement and not the terms set forth below. By installing, copying, or otherwise using the SOFTWARE PRODUCT, you agree to be bound by the terms of this EULA. If you do not agree to the terms of this EULA, you are not authorized to install, copy, or otherwise use the SOFTWARE PRODUCT; you may, however, return the SOFTWARE PRODUCT, along with all printed materials and other items that form a part of the Microsoft product that includes the SOFTWARE PRODUCT, to the place you obtained them for a full refund.

SOFTWARE PRODUCT LICENSE

The SOFTWARE PRODUCT is protected by United States copyright laws and international copyright treaties, as well as other intellectual property laws and treaties. The SOFTWARE PRODUCT is licensed, not sold.

1. **GRANT OF LICENSE.** This EULA grants you the following rights:

   a. **Software Product.** You may install and use one copy of the SOFTWARE PRODUCT on a single computer. The primary user of the computer on which the SOFTWARE PRODUCT is installed may make a second copy for his or her exclusive use on a portable computer.

   b. **Storage/Network Use.** You may also store or install a copy of the SOFTWARE PRODUCT on a storage device, such as a network server, used only to install or run the SOFTWARE PRODUCT on your other computers over an internal network; however, you must acquire and dedicate a license for each separate computer on which the SOFTWARE PRODUCT is installed or run from the storage device. A license for the SOFTWARE PRODUCT may not be shared or used concurrently on different computers.

   c. **License Pak.** If you have acquired this EULA in a Microsoft License Pak, you may make the number of additional copies of the computer software portion of the SOFTWARE PRODUCT authorized on the printed copy of this EULA, and you may use each copy in the manner specified above. You are also entitled to make a corresponding number of secondary copies for portable computer use as specified above.

   d. **Sample Code.** Solely with respect to portions, if any, of the SOFTWARE PRODUCT that are identified within the SOFTWARE PRODUCT as sample code (the "SAMPLE CODE"):

      i. **Use and Modification.** Microsoft grants you the right to use and modify the source code version of the SAMPLE CODE, *provided* you comply with subsection (d)(iii) below. You may not distribute the SAMPLE CODE, or any modified version of the SAMPLE CODE, in source code form.

      ii. **Redistributable Files.** Provided you comply with subsection (d)(iii) below, Microsoft grants you a nonexclusive, royalty-free right to reproduce and distribute the object code version of the SAMPLE CODE and of any modified SAMPLE CODE, other than SAMPLE CODE, or any modified version thereof, designated as not redistributable in the Readme file that forms a part of the SOFTWARE PRODUCT (the "Non-Redistributable Sample Code"). All SAMPLE CODE other than the Non-Redistributable Sample Code is collectively referred to as the "REDISTRIBUTABLES."

      iii. **Redistribution Requirements.** If you redistribute the REDISTRIBUTABLES, you agree to: (i) distribute the REDISTRIBUTABLES in object code form only in conjunction with and as a part of your software application product; (ii) not use Microsoft's name, logo, or trademarks to market your software application product; (iii) include a valid copyright notice on your software application product; (iv) indemnify, hold harmless, and defend Microsoft from and against any claims or lawsuits, including attorney's fees, that arise or result from the use or distribution of your software application product; and (v) not permit further distribution of the REDISTRIBUTABLES by your end user. Contact Microsoft for the applicable royalties due and other licensing terms for all other uses and/or distribution of the REDISTRIBUTABLES.

2. **DESCRIPTION OF OTHER RIGHTS AND LIMITATIONS.**

   - **Limitations on Reverse Engineering, Decompilation, and Disassembly.** You may not reverse engineer, decompile, or disassemble the SOFTWARE PRODUCT, except and only to the extent that such activity is expressly permitted by applicable law notwithstanding this limitation.

   - **Separation of Components.** The SOFTWARE PRODUCT is licensed as a single product. Its component parts may not be separated for use on more than one computer.

   - **Rental.** You may not rent, lease, or lend the SOFTWARE PRODUCT.

   - **Support Services.** Microsoft may, but is not obligated to, provide you with support services related to the SOFTWARE PRODUCT ("Support Services"). Use of Support Services is governed by the Microsoft policies and programs described in the user manual, in "online" documentation, and/or in other Microsoft-provided materials. Any supplemental software code provided to you as part of the Support Services shall be considered part of the SOFTWARE PRODUCT and subject to the terms and conditions of this EULA. With respect to technical information you provide to Microsoft as part of the Support Services, Microsoft may use such information for its business purposes, including for product support and development. Microsoft will not utilize such technical information in a form that personally identifies you.

   - **Software Transfer.** You may permanently transfer all of your rights under this EULA, provided you retain no copies, you transfer all of the SOFTWARE PRODUCT (including all component parts, the media and printed materials, any upgrades, this EULA, and, if applicable, the Certificate of Authenticity), **and** the recipient agrees to the terms of this EULA.

   - **Termination.** Without prejudice to any other rights, Microsoft may terminate this EULA if you fail to comply with the terms and conditions of this EULA. In such event, you must destroy all copies of the SOFTWARE PRODUCT and all of its component parts.

3. **COPYRIGHT.** All title and copyrights in and to the SOFTWARE PRODUCT (including but not limited to any images, photographs, animations, video, audio, music, text, SAMPLE CODE, REDISTRIBUTABLES, and "applets" incorporated into the SOFTWARE PRODUCT) and any copies of the SOFTWARE PRODUCT are owned by Microsoft or its suppliers. The SOFTWARE PRODUCT is protected by copyright laws and international treaty provisions. Therefore, you must treat the SOFTWARE PRODUCT like any other copyrighted material **except** that you may install the SOFTWARE PRODUCT on a single computer provided you keep the original solely for backup or archival purposes. You may not copy the printed materials accompanying the SOFTWARE PRODUCT.

4. **U.S. GOVERNMENT RESTRICTED RIGHTS.** The SOFTWARE PRODUCT and documentation are provided with RESTRICTED RIGHTS. Use, duplication, or disclosure by the Government is subject to restrictions as set forth in subparagraph (c)(1)(ii) of the Rights in Technical Data and Computer Software clause at DFARS 252.227-7013 or subparagraphs (c)(1) and (2) of the Commercial Computer Software—Restricted Rights at 48 CFR 52.227-19, as applicable. Manufacturer is Microsoft Corporation/One Microsoft Way/Redmond, WA 98052-6399.

5. **EXPORT RESTRICTIONS.** You agree that you will not export or re-export the SOFTWARE PRODUCT, any part thereof, or any process or service that is the direct product of the SOFTWARE PRODUCT (the foregoing collectively referred to as the "Restricted Components"), to any country, person, entity, or end user subject to U.S. export restrictions. You specifically agree not to export or re-export any of the Restricted Components (i) to any country to which the U.S. has embargoed or restricted the export of goods or services, which currently include, but are not necessarily limited to, Cuba, Iran, Iraq, Libya, North Korea, Sudan, and Syria, or to any national of any such country, wherever located, who intends to transmit or transport the Restricted Components back to such country; (ii) to any end user who you know or have reason to know will utilize the Restricted Components in the design, development, or production of nuclear, chemical, or biological weapons; or (iii) to any end user who has been prohibited from participating in U.S. export transactions by any federal agency of the U.S. government. You warrant and represent that neither the BXA nor any other U.S. federal agency has suspended, revoked, or denied your export privileges.

DISCLAIMER OF WARRANTY

NO WARRANTIES OR CONDITIONS. MICROSOFT EXPRESSLY DISCLAIMS ANY WARRANTY OR CONDITION FOR THE SOFT-WARE PRODUCT. THE SOFTWARE PRODUCT AND ANY RELATED DOCUMENTATION ARE PROVIDED "AS IS" WITHOUT WARRANTY OR CONDITION OF ANY KIND, EITHER EXPRESS OR IMPLIED, INCLUDING, WITHOUT LIMITATION, THE IMPLIED WARRANTIES OF MERCHANTABILITY, FITNESS FOR A PARTICULAR PURPOSE, OR NONINFRINGEMENT. THE ENTIRE RISK ARISING OUT OF USE OR PERFORMANCE OF THE SOFTWARE PRODUCT REMAINS WITH YOU.

LIMITATION OF LIABILITY. TO THE MAXIMUM EXTENT PERMITTED BY APPLICABLE LAW, IN NO EVENT SHALL MICROSOFT OR ITS SUPPLIERS BE LIABLE FOR ANY SPECIAL, INCIDENTAL, INDIRECT, OR CONSEQUENTIAL DAMAGES WHATSOEVER (INCLUDING, WITHOUT LIMITATION, DAMAGES FOR LOSS OF BUSINESS PROFITS, BUSINESS INTERRUPTION, LOSS OF BUSINESS INFORMATION, OR ANY OTHER PECUNIARY LOSS) ARISING OUT OF THE USE OF OR INABILITY TO USE THE SOFTWARE PRODUCT OR THE PROVISION OF OR FAILURE TO PROVIDE SUPPORT SERVICES, EVEN IF MICROSOFT HAS BEEN ADVISED OF THE POSSIBILITY OF SUCH DAMAGES. IN ANY CASE, MICROSOFT'S ENTIRE LIABILITY UNDER ANY PROVISION OF THIS EULA SHALL BE LIMITED TO THE GREATER OF THE AMOUNT ACTUALLY PAID BY YOU FOR THE SOFTWARE PRODUCT OR US$5.00; PROVIDED, HOWEVER, IF YOU HAVE ENTERED INTO A MICROSOFT SUPPORT SERVICES AGREEMENT, MICROSOFT'S ENTIRE LIABILITY REGARDING SUPPORT SERVICES SHALL BE GOVERNED BY THE TERMS OF THAT AGREE-MENT. BECAUSE SOME STATES AND JURISDICTIONS DO NOT ALLOW THE EXCLUSION OR LIMITATION OF LIABILITY, THE ABOVE LIMITATION MAY NOT APPLY TO YOU.

MISCELLANEOUS

This EULA is governed by the laws of the State of Washington USA, except and only to the extent that applicable law mandates governing law of a different jurisdiction.

Should you have any questions concerning this EULA, or if you desire to contact Microsoft for any reason, please contact the Microsoft subsidiary serving your country, or write: Microsoft Sales Information Center/One Microsoft Way/Redmond, WA 98052-6399.

Proof of Purchase

0-7356-0975-6

Do not send this card with your registration.
Use this card as proof of purchase if participating in a promotion or
rebate offer on *Microsoft® FrontPage® 2000 Step by Step Courseware Core Skills Student Guide*. Card
must be used in conjunction with other proof(s) of payment such as your dated sales receipt—
see offer details.

Microsoft® FrontPage® 2000 Step by Step Courseware
Core Skills Student Guide

WHERE DID YOU PURCHASE THIS PRODUCT?

CUSTOMER NAME

Microsoft®Press
mspress.microsoft.com

Microsoft Press, PO Box 97017, Redmond, WA 98073-9830

OWNER REGISTRATION CARD **Register Today!** 0-7356-0975-6

Return the bottom portion of this card to register today.

Microsoft® FrontPage® 2000 Step by Step Courseware
Core Skills Student Guide

FIRST NAME   MIDDLE INITIAL   LAST NAME

INSTITUTION OR COMPANY NAME

ADDRESS

CITY   STATE   ZIP

( )

E-MAIL ADDRESS   PHONE NUMBER

U.S. and Canada addresses only. Fill in information above and mail postage-free.
Please mail only the bottom half of this page.

For information about Microsoft Press®
products, visit our Web site at
mspress.microsoft.com

Microsoft·*Press*